The American Sublime

The American Sublime

Edited by
MARY ARENSBERG

State University of New York Press

Published by
State University of New York Press, Albany

For information, address State University of New York Press, State University Plaza, Albany, N.Y., 12246

Library of Congress Cataloging in Publication Data

The American Sublime.

Includes bibliographies and index.

1. American poetry—History and criticism—Addresses, essays, lectures. 2. Sublime, The, in literature—Addresses, essays, lectures. 3. Dickinson, Emily, 1830–1886—Criticism and interpretation—Addresses, essays, lectures. 4 Stevens, Wallace, 1879–1955—Criticism and interpretation—Addresses, essays, lectures. I. Arensberg, Mary, 1945–

PS310.S87A44 1986 811'.009 85-31824

ISBN 0-88706-189-3

ISBN 0-88706-190-7 (pbk.)

For

James Baird
Hugh Maclean
Helen Regueiro Elam

Contents

Acknowledgments

The idea for this collection was germinated in an old fashioned seminar room in Thames Hall on the Connecticut College campus many years ago. As the spring rain misted the apple blossoms outside, inside we discussed "supreme fictions," particularly those of the American poets Whitman, Dickinson and Wallace Stevens. Later there was the "American Sublime" of Harold Bloom whose "capable imagination" revised our poetic canon through those "negative moments" or sublime crossings mapped out in this volume. I am also indebted to the following colleagues and relatives whose support and intelligence were invaluable: Professors Sara Schyfter, Sarah Blacher Cohen, Eugene Garber, Donald Stauffer, Aaron Rosenblatt, Harry Staley, Randall Craig, Mary Anne Sullivan Devane, Helen Desfosses, Elizabeth Wilson; Elizabeth, Tom and Barbara Blatner and my son, Phillip.

Chapter 1

Introduction: The American Sublime

MARY ARENSBERG

Ghostlike we glide through nature,
and should not know our place again

--Emerson

In one of his last poems, Wallace Stevens assumes the cloak of Ulysses to speak about the quest of all wandering poets: the search for the "sublime." He envisions the sublime as an "englistered woman . . . seen/in an isolation, separate from the human in humanity,/a part of the inhuman more,/The still inhuman more." Yet she remains a metaphor, an image for something that cannot be named, precisely because the sublime is the inhuman, the realm of things beyond ourselves, the dimension of otherness we can never know. Not finding her in human form, not even in the patience of Penelope, Stevens-Ulysses sets sail once more, seeking a voice, a way of knowing beyond the human threshold. *Limen*, boundary or threshold from the Latin, is both the etymological and philosophical root of the sublime.[1] Poems get written, then, because that threshold has never been crossed or articulated; for to trangress that boundary, to speak with the tongue of a god would be to achieve the sublime and also silence.

The Romantic Sublime of Keats, Shelley, and Wordsworth was preoccupied with crossings between self and nature—what they called transcendence—and with the boundlessness of the universe or a field of daffodils. Yet, in his stunning account, *The Romantic Sublime: Studies in the Structure and Psychology of Transcendence,* Thomas Weiskel suggests that since we "live in an age when we have lost the obsession with natural infinitude" and can look back at our earth from the vantage of a space vehicle, the idea of a sublime may well be a "moribund aesthetic." He goes on to demonstrate that in "contemporary criticism and the development of structuralist thinking as well, we learn how very little of our creations belongs to individual vision and choice."[2] We live in a place that is increasingly finite, limited, and, as Stevens said, "not our own." Ten years have passed since Weiskel's own death and this pronouncement; since then, not only has our sense of the heavens diminished, but also, our sense of ourselves.

The past decade in American literary criticism has confirmed Weiskel's perceptions: even as the Star Wars project threatens to crowd the void of outer space, so the literary enterprise known as "deconstruction" undermines the notions of Self, Nature, Imagination, Truth, Reality, constructs formerly identified with the Romantic sublime. Since the importation of Jacques Derrida's deconstruction into this country by the Yale School critics, J. Hillis Miller and Paul deMan, and numerous misreadings of Derridean practice by American critics, the "ultimate truths" of language (Self, God, Essence, and so on) have been called into question. No longer do some of us view language signs as absolutes or transcendental signifieds.[3] Instead, these former anchors of meaning have been cast back into the vast sea of textuality where no word or sign is privileged over any other: "freedom is just another word" and, in fact, a fiction invented through the free play of other words and signs. The sublime, too, in poststructuralist thinking, becomes a fiction for transcendence, itself a fiction of absolute disclosure. However, within the free play of language and its various scenes, the sublime is alive and doing well, although it may be living under the guise of assumed names. This collection of essays is an inquiry into those assumed names: how to identify those American texts which open up a quest for the sublime, and particularly, how to read sublimity in the poststructuralist mode.

It is necessary to begin with "Longinus," whose third century *Peri Hypsos (On Great Writing)*, is the origin or at least the beginning of the tradition of the sublime. His text opens up the question of the sublime as a linguistic effect by stating that: "Sublimity is always an eminence and excellence in language."[4] The Longinian sublime is essentially rhetorical and identified as the reader's response to great utterance. "For it is a fact of Nature that the soul is raised by true Sublimity, it gains a proud flight upwards, it is filled with joy and exhultation, as though itself had produced what it hears." The crucial words in this passage, *as though*, suggest that even in this ancient reader's sublime, the moment of sublimity is always a language scene which produces an uncanny metaphorical effect. Affect, however, the emotional response, is attributed to the "reader" who experiences not a *déjà vu* but a *déjà écrit*: it seems as if she has written what she has heard. Yet, even as he grounds his sublime in language, Longinus goes on to describe an extra-linguistic or affective aim: "Sublimity . . . parts all matter this way and that, and like a lightning flash, reveals, at a stroke and in its entirety, the power of the orator." In these few passages, Longinus supplies us with several of the rhetorical and psychologic structures which inform the problematic of the sublime, ancient or modern:

1. The experience of the sublime is an affective or emotional response (joy and ecstasy) to **power, authenticity** or **authority.**

2. This **power** is perceived in a moment (like a "lightning flash") through the effects of speech and language.

3. The sublime moment is preceded by a disruption in normal consciousness ("parts all matter this way and that") whose equilibrium must be restored.

4. Equilibrium is seemingly restored through an identification with that **power** or **authority** ("exhalts our soul as though we had created what we merely heard") and a **repression** of that power.

5. The repression takes the form of a **defense** (in this case **mimesis**) in which the reader makes the sublime her own.

To some readers, this outline of the Longinian sublime may seem uncannily familiar: as Neil Hertz has brilliantly pointed out, there are the elements of an Oedipal conflict inherent in the reader's confrontation with great writing, and we can also detect the sketchy patterns of Harold Bloom's readings of the sublime and its relationship to literary influence.[5] Finally, the Longinian sublime is also suggestive of other poststructuralist theories of language which discount the referential capacity of words or signs and deny that meaning is immediately present in language. Already in Longinus, the sublime is a trope, a metaphor, which includes both its rhetorical elements (subject, reader, poet and object, text, discourse), as well as its psychological strain or the experiential response to great language.

Although the Longianian sublime articulates the "problem," the modern or negative sublime finds its full expression in Kant's *Critique of Judgement*. Yet the bridge between the ancient reader's sublime and the Kantian drama of the imagination is the eighteenth century which retrieved "Longinus" from the ancients and foraged his version of sublimity for its own purposes. Addison and Burke were the first to distinguish between the sublime and the beautiful; since then, the beautiful is reserved for positive qualities, while the sublime is linked with emotions of displeasure such as anxiety, panic, and terror. Evoked by moments of extreme aphasia or disorientation, the "sublime," according to Bruce Clarke, "tends to break continuities and open epistemological gaps."[6] Thus the eighteenth century sublime becomes obsessed, not with the moment of restored power or identification, but with the moment of breaking or the experience of discontinuity that precedes the sublimatory act.

Concurrent with this positioning of anxiety as the central emotional response to the sublime by Burke, particularly, was the Lockean notion of anxiety elicited by the perception of absence. Locke, of course, was concerned with the absence of the soul, the empty vessel, which becomes, in more modern versions of the sublime, the nothingness of the self and the perceived loss of the Other. Absence and anxiety, the twin affective strains of the eighteenth century sublime, displace the Longinian emotions of joy and exhaltation, to become the central participants in Kant's drama, and, in fact, define its psychologic structure.

Kant's scenario of the sublime is divided into two types: the first is the **mathematical** sublime that may be described as the imagination's inability to grasp magnitude or endless progressions; the second, the **dynamical** sublime, is concerned with the effect of power on the imagination. In both instances, the psychic operation fictionalized by Kant occurs within the mind of the subject without the direct participation of the object; the object merely exists to initiate the psychic response. Unlike the Longinian sublime, in which the object is subsumed by the subject, in the Kantian version, the object is seemingly erased while reason is privileged over the imaginative or psychodynamic faculty.

Weiskel has outlined the three phases of the Kantian models.[7] In the first phase, the mind and object are in a determinate relationship; there is a smooth correspondence between inside and out, and equilibrium is maintained. During the second phase, however, the normal relationship between subject and object is destroyed, and either the subject or object is suddenly in excess. This moment of disorientation may occur at any time in response to a phenomenon in nature, perhaps a line of poetry or even an unconscious memory. It is as though there were an anxiety attack engendered on the imagination resulting in displeasure and unease. In the third and final phase, equilibrium is restored through the mind's "constituting a fresh relation between itself and the object such that the very indeterminacy which erupted in phase two is taken as symbolizing the mind's relation to a transcendent order."[8] In other words, sublimation occurs when reason comes to rescue the tottering imagination to restore the primacy of reason and its limitations. The fall into reason makes the abyss of magnitude or power symbolically cognate with the infinitude or abyss of the human mind.

Two fictional psychic functions are disclosed in this outline: first is the collapse of the imaginative faculty, and second, the aggrandizing of reason which is called on to reconstitute the psychic balance. Precipitated by an imagined excess in the object, the subject's crisis emerges from a fear of being engulfed; to dissuade the anxiety, the subject evolves a reaction formation or psychic defense. In this defense, the imagination is repressed and reason emerges as psychic victor. It is not difficult to transpose Kant's formulations into a Freudian psychodrama in which the subject becomes the ego; the object, the Other; while reason is a hypothetical superego. The ego, in the first stages of the sublime, is threatened by a surplus of stimulation from the object and experiences fear of injury (castration) or power (incorporation). "This anxiety is met by a reaction formation . . . which precipitates a recapitulation of the Oedipus Complex; this in turn yields to a feeling of guilt (superego anxiety) and is resolved through identification (introjection)."[9] Although this scheme, which follows Wieskel's guidelines for a Freudian sublime, is inherently reductive, it does demonstrate the natural progression from the Kantian account of negative sublimity to versions of the modern sublime grounded in both Kant and Freud.

The critic who has perpetually mused on Freud and the sublime is Harold Bloom. *In Poetry and Repression* and *Agon: Towards a Theory of Revisionism*, particularly, Bloom articulates Freud's "enormous importance in the history of the sublime" and then constructs his own theories of literary influence and sublimity from the Freudian models.[10] Bloom reads Freud as "the last great theorist of that (sublime) mode," and calls the essay on "The Uncanny": "the only major contribution that the twentieth century has made to the aesthetics of the sublime." Reading the essay in what he calls his antithetical stance, Bloom discloses Freud's true subject (one he has repressed) as the sublime rather than the uncanny.

> Anxieties when confronted with anterior powers are overtly the concerns of the essay on "the uncanny." E. T. Hoffman's *The Sand Man* provides Freud with his text, and for once Freud allows himself to be a very useful practical critic of an imaginative story. The repetition-compulsion . . . brilliantly is invoked to open up what is hidden in the story. Uncanniness is traced back to the narcisscistic belief in "omnipotence of thought" which in aesthetic terms is necessarily the power of the mind over the universe of the senses and death.[11]

In this passage, Bloom links the sublime with narcissism and repression, the centerpieces of his own theories of literary history and intertextuality, at the same time he represses the tradition of the sublime ("anxieties when confronted with anterior powers") to make a space for his own. Omnipotence of thought, or the neurotic illusion that we can think something into being, is transposed by Freud-Bloom into the third or restorative phase of the scenario of the sublime.

Other of Bloom's "misreadings" of Freud, which turn on the theories of the primal scene and the family romance, eventuate into his six-part rhetorical psychology of poetic origins, genealogy, and the sublime.[12] The story begins with the post-Enlightenment's "strong" poetry, Milton and after, where the young poet (ephebe), having initially fixated on and primally repressed the power of a strong precursor-poet, chooses his/her own counter-sublime to combat the perceived "threat." Finding his/her own voice through a repression of the "father" poet, the seemingly liberated ephebe can finally identify with the precursor through acts of misreading the antecedent's text. "Three times the strong latecomer contracts and withdraws himself, experiencing a 'negative moment' followed by a 'crossing' over into expansive acts of positive self-representation."[13] Yet, in the final stage, the revision is so complete, it seems as if the ephebe had written what the poetic father had indeed created. Bloom's own counter-sublime here sounds uncannily familier, a misreading of Burke, Kant, and Freud; however, like his true precursor, Longinus, he opens up the problem of the sublime "yet once more."

II

> There is no outside, no enclosing wall, no circumference to us.
>
> Emerson, "Circles"

When we move from the two Kantian sublimes, which inform and structure the British Romantic sublime, to the American sublime, there is still the problem of nature's surplus signification (its vastness and infinitudes), and there remain the problems of "belatedness' and the self. American poetics has been radicalized in recent years by such antithetical readers as Harold Bloom and John Irwin.[14] Emphasis has shifted from Adamic models of American romanticism with their virgin landscapes and notions of prelapsarian, unmediated vision to a dramatic scenario of an American counter-sublime. The epic solipsism, myths of the self, discussed by earlier readers of *Leaves of Grass* and *Paterson*, has been displaced by revisionist theories of intertextuality which replay and ground the poets of the American sublime against their Romantic precursors. In its revisionist incarnation, the American self of the traditional Emerson dissolves, splintering into what Bloom calls a "self-rebetting" of the self. Tracing an almost exclusively patrilineal line that begins with Emerson and ends, right now, with Ammons and Ashbery, Bloom has fathered a version of the American sublime which downplays rather than registers the importance of the precursor. The American sublime, according to Bloom, "begins anew not with the restoration or rebirth . . . of the Wordsworthian Sublime, but that is truly past such displacement."[15] Instead, the American sublime is a merger, a blending of the poetic self with the fathering force of an anterior power. Bloom's own assumption, which distinguishes his theories from those of the deconstructionists, is that there is a self, a tangible voice, which in Emerson cries out "I and the Abyss."

A strong contender for the most sublime passage in the American canon is Ishmael's discourse on the whiteness of the whale in *Moby Dick.*

> Is it by its indefiniteness it shadows forth the heartless voids and immensities of the universe, and thus stabs us from behind with the thought of annihiliaiton, when beholding the white depths of the Milky Way? Or is it that as in essence whiteness is not so much a color as the visible absence of color, and at the same time the concrete of all colors; is it for all these reasons that there is such a dumb blankness, full of meaning in a wide landscape of snows—a colorless, all color of atheism from which we shrink . . . so the wretched infidel gazes himself blind at the monumental white shroud that wraps all the prospect around him.[16]

Here Ishmael's anxiety stems not so much from the "heartless voids" and immensities of the universe that proves so threatening to his English Romantic precursors, but from the "dumb blankness" of the whale that mirrors the abyss of himself. Melville's version of the psychodrama of the sublime is not resolved through a cathartic identification between outside and inside as in the Kantian drama, nor is there a return to an Oedipal confrontation and introjection of the rival. In the American brand of sublimity, the imagination finds itself the inhabitant of a place that is not its own, a vortex of atheism, which Wallace Stevens later called "the empty spirit/In vacant space." Excluded from its own nature and shrinking from the white depths of nature's abyss, the American self is the "dumb blankness," the deconstructed self. This nothingness of the American self may be traced from Emerson's trope, "the transparent eyeball" ("I am nothing; I see all") up through Stevens' "snow man" who, "nothing himself, beholds nothing that is not there, and the nothing there is." Yet, unlike the snowman who reads nothing in the sound of the wind, the American poet is fixated on the whiteness of his/her surroundings: Dickinson cloaking herself in only white, Melville scribbling its meanings on the white whale as text.

The incantation of whiteness and the American sublime is also present in Frost's sonnet, "Design."

> I found a dimpled spider, fat and white
> On a white heal-all, holding up a moth
> Like a white piece of rigid satin cloth—
> Assorted characters of death and blight
> Mixed ready to begin the morning right
> Like the ingredients of a witch's broth—
> A snow-drop spider, a flower like a froth,
> And dead wings carried like a paper kite.
>
> What had that flower to do with being white,
> The wayside blue and innocent heal-all?
> What brought that kindred spider to that height,
> Then steered the white moth thither in the night?
> What but design of darkness to appall?—
> If design govern in a thing so small?[17]

Conventional readings of the Frost text are as innocent as its white heal-all. Readers are apt to interpret the sonnet as a conceit personifying the horrors of nature which is governed by some malevolent power beyond our control. In the sestet, the speaker has witnessed a sinister little drama in the natural world and wonders, if the powers of darkness, blind fate, can operate so sadistically in the microcosm, what deviltry can they be enacting in the macro work? Two critical assumptions inform this interpretation: the first is that the speaker has actually seen nature's macabre design and is haunted by its implications as global synecdoche; or, if he has invented the scene, it represents the presence of what Emerson called "Necessity" and we call "providence" in the material world. "The world is emblematic," writes Emerson in "Nature," and this Frost text seems to metaphorize the presence of a dark fate at work in this universe of death and blight.

Recent criticism, however, particularly the antithetical practices of Bloom, cues us to suspect the surface of a text. Texts, like psyches, may say one thing while they mean another, or else repress their true meaning through defensive psychic strategies. Readers of the Frost poem are lured to forget one simple fact; that what the speaker has seen is nothing, that he encounters nature as whiteness or absence. Frost's tableau of a white spider placed on a white heal-all holding up a snowy moth like "a piece of rigid satin cloth" is truly emblematic of a major strain of the American sublime: the incantation of whiteness as a figure for the alienation one feels toward nature (the encounter with nothingess) and the emptiness of the vessel of the self. Inflicted like Ishmael with the snowman syndrome or the "dumb blankness" within and without, the American poet is appalled by the absence encountered and instead settles for the white shroud of metaphor (the invention of nature) that veils the abyss. However, Melville's and perhaps Frost's deconstructions of nature and self do not end in the substitution of a fiction. For as Ishmael points out, even nature's effort to cover over the "charnel house within" ("Nature absolutely paints like a harlot":) is a cosmetic that turns itself on the white and colorless principle of light.

What Roy Harvey Pearce calls the "primary egocentricism" and later commentators term the "radical solipsism" of the American sublime begins with the antinomian,

Adamic principles of our sublime's great white father, Emerson. This collection opens with Donald Pease's essay, "Sublime Politics," which provides an excursion through the history of the sublime (via Monk, Kant, Hayden White, and Thomas Weiskel) to focus on the movement of modernism "where history ends with the permanent resolution of the sign." In the end, Pease finally comes to rest on Emerson whose version of the sublime is ahistorical and unable to be superseded. For unlike the Kantian drama, where nature's power necessitates the intervention of reason at the expense of the imagination, or the egotistical sublime where the self's will to power triumphs over nature the devourer, Emerson's sublime strikes a balance. Rather it is a figure of place, a *topos*, which opens up a passage between self and world where the sublime is always about to take place. Citing the text of the "transparent eyeball" as the central scene of this fictional confluence, Pease then focuses on the person "crossing bare common" as the figure that represents the breach between otherness and self.

In the Pease reading, this speaker unfolds into the dual figure of the child who desires a world of things and not ideas and the American idealist whose ideas provided the rationale for the rape of the American landscape. And here, the dialogue between the two aspects of the American sublime breaks down, before the discontinuities between ideas and things, self and other may be articulated into yet another irresolution. Like "the transparent eyeball" which can never register an image because of its opaqueness, the breakdown of the dialogue metaphorizes the impossibility of achieving a sublime at the same time it perpetuates the quest. For Pease, the history of the sublime conforms to this repetitive pattern of irresolution: as one discipline is about to perfect a sublime, another is there to displace its ideas and usurp its place. In this way, Pease links the discourse of modernism (the desire to be at the end of history) with the dialectic of the history of the sublime: both are misread into history in the infinite turnings of language, the surpassing and repressing that makes possible a clearing in the dark.

As Geoffrey Hartman observes in *Criticism in the Wilderness*, the American poet's obsession to purify language is an enjoyable exercise in exploiting "the thought that it can't be done."[18] Like Stevens' "Man on the Dump," "sitting among the mattresses of the dead," the American poet is positioned on the detritus of worn out images, the trash heap of Emerson's "perpetual allegories" with no way to climb down. The American poet discovers that what he beats out "on an old tin can or lard pail" is the song of the self, itself a construct of language trash. In Joseph Kronick's reading of Whitman's sublime, "On the Borders of History: Whitman and the American Sublime," Emerson's paradigm of "I and the Abyss" becomes a paradoxical equation: the I is the Abyss and the Abyss is language. However, by language this critic means the inscriptions of the past which make possible the fictions of the self. As Kronick explains, "the text of the self is a reading of the past that lies before one." The American sublime here is not to imagine a new idea under the sun or to enact a Bloomian misreading of a precursor, but rather to cross the border of the text to reappropriate the past, and "thus meet one's own death."

Walt Whitman, following Emerson's directive toward linguistic organicism (the integration of language with nature) attempts a radical return to "origins" through etymological excursions. In fact, Whitman's methods of indirection that rescue the poetical in language prevent the possibility of that return. For the poet's use of slang is both "a swerving away from America's European background" and yet a return to the original metaphoricity of primal language. However, a turning toward the ur-tropical landscape of language is in fact a turn away from its origins; and, as Kronick points out, "by thus undermining the concept of originality, Whitman opens up a space for himself as an American writer." In his willful dislocation of the text from the linearity of history, Whitman is able to enter the patrilineal line of American poets who strive to "make it new." Poems such as "Passage to India" and "Out of the Cradle Endlessly Rocking" are sea voyages that attempt to transgress the margins of history. Yet, it is their failure to reach beyond the shores of writing that keeps these texts afloat. In their endless paths of circumnavigation toward a primal scene of language, these texts disclose an origin now vanished, submerged like Atlantis, beyond the borders of history.

Emily Dickinson's counter-sublime consists of self-made strategies invented to combat both the authority of the American poetic patriarchy and also the power of nature or the outside. In response to Emerson's dualistic fictions of the Me and the Not Me, Dickinson, according to Joanne Feit Diehl, "creates a conception of authority that re-places herself at the center of a self-made world." Instead of perpetuating the division of self and other, she creates a vortex of self and world (the vital I) that erases any notion of an outside and empowers her own sublime. At times she does conceive of otherness as a male adversary haunting her universe; however, when she experiences the other as feminine, the chill of competition vanishes. For Dickinson, the woman-to-woman encounter provides a circumference of female magic that shields the "vital I and assuages the anxieties of the masculine influence.

Kant's analytic of the sublime distinguishes two types of experiential sublimity: the dynamical sublime in which the mind is seemingly terrorized by its own contemplation of an external source; and the mathematical sublime, the inability of the mind to encompass infinitude. Although both sublimes are negative moments threatening the loss of identity, their corresponding stages of blockage are gauged to restore "the Unitary status of the self." In the identificatory drama of the romantic sublime (the Kant-Weiskel models), "the superogatory strength of investment that turns the Superego (Reason) into a harsher taskmaster than the father, there eventuates the problem of excess." Can all the anxiety connected with the sublime encounter be displaced on the other (reason, father, superego), or is there an excess which, in Derrida's terms, "cannot be brought back to the father?" Weiskel displaces the excess into the pre-Oedipal or maternal sphere; but, as Helen Regueiro suggests, that identification with the mother (Eve) is itself a negative moment "beset by the otherness which it attempts to heal."

Dickinson's poems in Regueiro's essay, are haunted by that otherness which they try to overcome. These texts, themselves cryptograms of breakage, disclose the impossibility of their own gestures and never do achieve wholeness. Sublimity, in the Dickinsonian vision, occurs not when "coincidence" of self and other converge, but in those times of darkness, when the abyss is illuminated not by the light, but in the depths of its own darkness.

Narcissistic doubling becomes the idiom of her texts, and instead of finding wholeness, when the self is at one with itself, she experiences self loss. There are "visions of wholeness" when nature and self coincide, but sublimity is always a negative moment that occurs in a state of crisis, a paradoxical instance of simultaneous voicing and silence, of a "seeing" into the dark.

In reckoning with the darkness that circumscribes her poems, Dickinson's other strategy, according to Gary Lee Stonum, is to engage in combat (power poetry) against the forces of the outside. However, unlike her male counterparts whose wrestling is with the daemonic angel of the precursor's text, or with the demons of the perceived external world, Dickinson wrests power from the other by staging a power ploy all her own. In registering her will to power over a universe of death and other texts, she practices a singular poetic Stonum calls "the calculated sublime." Through a series of mathematical metaphors which reapportion the world inherited from Emerson, "Dickinson's computations aggressively rearrange the existing world and established ideas of it."

Her poetics of power, a self-rebetting achieved within a circumference she inscribes for herself, is augmented and magnified by her fictitious calculations. Stonum will not go so far as to nominate Dickinson as a poet of the sublime. But in her mathematical poems that invent a realm of habitable fictions, Dickinson traces the outlines of the abyssal center and measures the distance between herself and "the apocalyptic realm."

From his "paltry nude" moving noiselessly out to the center of "sea-green pomp" to the patient Penelope "waiting for him that comes constantly so near," Wallace Stevens expresses his counter-sublime as a muse attachment. He calls her his interior paramour. Stevens is so belated a poet that for him the sublime is already a fiction, an effect of rhetoric with no reference to an experience outside the text. And yet, as Michael Beehler demonstrates, there is in the Stevens' canon "a dynamics of the sublime" that mimics the quest of all poets for that place beyond the horizon where poetry cannot proceed. And as a figure within the text itself, the sublime (irrational) takes a place within the poetry as it refers to the irrational outside the text. Thus, "the irrational appears as a process that erases the boundary between inside and outside by allowing it to be written only as a metaphor of boundary."

Beehler opens with Kant's sublime which he terms "a journey to the boundary of representation." Stevens's sublime begins at that edge, where representation is deemed an impossibility and the sublime becomes a trope. As perhaps the first of the deconstructive critics, Stevens's misreading of Kant undermines the vital boundary beyond which metaphor can pass, freeing all words and signs from signification into a text that is merely "a theatre of trope." Beehler's own deconstructive reading of Stevens's sublime traces the explorers in Stevens's poetry "whose journeys disclose the metaphoric margin that allows their figurative passage to take place." In Stevens, the margin is already a fiction, a metaphor of margin. As he writes at the end of his great epic on the impossibility of a sublime, *Notes Towards A Supreme Fiction*: "They will get it right one day at the Sorbonne/We shall return at twilight from a lecture/Pleased that the irrational is rational." In this proleptic vision of the deconstructive criticism of our own time, Stevens's uncanny insights here point toward the poststructuralist sublime.

Perhaps the most sublime moment in Stevens's poetry is his meditation on the aurora borealis, "The Auroras of Autumn," which moves the American sublime "into the great Sunset of Selfhood in the evening land." Stevens's questor for the sublime or, as he calls it, "the supreme fiction," is the figure of "our man," or the masculine other of the rhetorical "we" that populates his poetry. Sired by "the timeless mother" in the beginning of his first volume of poetry, *Harmonium*, the poet-son is never able to satisfy the yearning love for the original parent. Instead, he invents a fictive mate who (n)ever takes her place; and this second woman, the interior paramour, persists throughout the canon until usurped by another maternal substitute, the haunted muse or death-mother. The third muse, like memory, is the silent goddess of death whose sublimity is achieved through the force of her absence. She is a trace for that otherness (the sublime) whose presence was an illusion.

In the terror and isolation of the auroral scene, the poet is seized, like Ishmael, by the "white mythology" of the American sublime. Not usually recognized as a ephebe of Freud, Stevens is indeed obsessed with the impossible fantasy of the primal scene and the inevitable blankness of a place that never was. Although a fictional topos, aware of its status as syntactic event, the Stevensian moment of sublimity occurs as an erasure, a whiting out of the family romance. As the parental space and memory itself are seemingly obliterated and estranged from the past, the poet is faced with the whiteness that makes possible the fiction of the abyss. The fictional moment of sublimity in Stevens is the sublime as salvation and suicide, as the poet loses an identity he knows he never possessed.

In the various models of the sublime, the male company of poets resolves its experience of discontinuity either through an alignment with "the patrilineal voices of authority" or with the power of reason or the reconstituted self. However, as Diehl points out, the woman poet in the face of the sublime is beset by even more problems than her male counterparts. Barred from a tradition of male poets whose voices drown out the poems of her gender, unable to enact an Oedipal identification with a strong male precursor or to trope on the feminine other as muse, the "woman poet . . . becomes either silenced by the incursion of the sublime or radicalized by the process."

Emily Dickinson wrests power for her own through a radical deconstruction of her father's ground. However, Dickinson is our strongest exception, but other women poets, such as H.D., Marianne Moore, Adrienne Rich, and Elizabeth Bishop, approach the sublime obscurely and through paths of sublimation. Moore and H.D., who perceive their texts, much less themselves, as living in a place that is not their own, devise a poetics of encoded meanings that disguises their gestures toward an alternative feminine sublime. Adrienne Rich confronts the male-dominated tradition both directly and indirectly: in her reassertion of a daughter or woman-to-woman relationship as the ground of poetic indebtedness, she points directly toward an alternate sublime. But in her poems that "whisper" and verge on the silence of pure poetry so sought after by male poets, her texts founder on the very problematics of the masculine tradition from which she finds strength and yet eschews.

Both Rich and Bishop exemplify the "twilight" moments of the American sublime. For them, the Adamic self and the visions of Emerson's and Stevens's "giants of reality" must give way to the words of a second Eve whose daughters will found another earth, a second myth from which their poems will spring. In Bishop's texts, the overt sexual presence felt so strongly in Whitman and even in Stevens is dismissed to admit an asexual voice whose authority is grounded in a Me that renounces all gender.

In his concluding essay in *Agon*, Harold Bloom instructs "the American critic" to "keep faith with American poetry and the American Negative, which means not to yield to the School of Deconstruction or the perpetual school of British Common Sense." The results of this advice, he believes, will be a "mixed discourse, perhaps vatic, and at once esoteric and democratic, but that is often the burden of the American tradition."[18] The essays in this collection would seem to follow Bloom's dicta, in spirit if not in the letter. Some of the essays do yield to the School of Deconstruction; others offer a mixed discourse as they trace central American poetic scenes: the "transparency" of Emerson's eyeball; Whitman's "passage" to India; Dickinson's charting the circumference and encounter with the "caverns" of the soul; or Stevens's gazing at death in the auroras. At times, the American sublime is a struggle with other poets: a strong daughter wresting power from her father to make a clearing of her own. At other times, the sublime is a struggle with Otherness: the silence of a "wide landscape of snows" or the ghostliness of the haunted muse. Yet the idea of the sublime is certainly not a moribund aesthetic, but, like Ishmael awash on the bark of Queequeg's coffin. the American sublime survives, alone to tell the darker thread of the story.

Notes

1. Literally the sublime, *sub limen*, under the threshold, links etymologically with notions of threshold, lintel, boundary, margin, ground, and oblique, as well as with sublimination: subliminal.

2. Thomas Weiskel, *The Romantic Sublime* (Baltimore: The Johns Hopkins University Press, 1976), 6. This introduction, as well as all contemporary readings of the sublime, is informed and enhanced by Weiskel's brilliant book.

3. A term of Derrida's that refers to the absolutes of the Western language tradition: God, the world, the self. In deconstruction, these words are merely signifiers pointing toward, but never signifying, notions outside the text.

4. All references to Longinus are to "On the Sublime" translated by A. O. Pritchard, in *Criticism: The Rational Statement*, edited by Charles Kaplan (New York: St. Martin's Press, 1975), 54–93.

5. See particularly, Neil Hetz, "A Reading of Longinia" *Critical Inquiry*, (March 1983) and Harold Bloom, *A Map of Misleading* (New York: Oxford University Press, 1975); *Poetry and Repression* (New Haven: Yale University Press, 1976); and *Agon: Towards a Theory of Revisionism*) New York: Oxford University Press, 1982).

6. Bruce Clarke, "Sublimination and Sublimity-in 'home at Grasmere,' " *Studies in Romanticism* 19; 3 (Fall 1980).

7. See Weiskel, 39ff. Weiskel's discussion of the Kantian sublime reoccurs throughout his text.

8. Weiskel, 105.

9. See especially *Agon* and *The Breaking of the Vessels* (Chicago: University of Chicago Press, 1982).

10. Bloom, *Agon*, 102.

11. Vincent B. Leitch, *Deconstructive Criticism: An Advanced Introduction* (New York: Columbia University Press, 1983), 135.

12. Ibid.

13. Ibid.

14. See John T. Irwin's, *American Hieroglyphics: The Symbol of the Egyptian Hieroglyphics in American Renaissance* (New Haven: Yale University Press, 1980).

15. Bloom, *Agon*, 104.

16. Herman Melville, *Moby Dick* (New York: Houghton Miffin, 1968).

17. Robert Frost, "Design" in *The Poetry of Robert Frost*, edited by E. C. Lathem (New York: Holt Rinehard Winston, 1967), 153.

18. Bloom, *Agon*, 395.

Chapter 2

Sublime Politics

DONALD PEASE

In his fine study of the eighteenth century's changing attitude toward the sublime, Samuel Holt Monk indirectly registers his respect for his subject by discovering his finest moments of eloquence in registering his inability to provide a conclusive final chapter. Unable adequately either to define the term or to circumscribe the experience underwritten by it, Monk accepts the diminished task of locating the precondition for its historical appearance. In Monk's historical narrative, the sublime, through a strategic alliance with its opposite, the beautiful, effected the displacement of rhetoric by aesthetics as the dominant eighteenth-century cultural discipline. But even as it oversaw this interdisciplinary rebellion, the sublime seemed answerable to neither of the antagonists. Less a rhetorical or even an aesthetic category so much as a power to make trouble for categorizing procedures, the sublime, according to Monk's description, marked the gathering place for all "the elements in art that the Cartesian aesthetic had suppressed or not accounted for." Given this analysis of the sublime effect, it is no wonder Monk surrendered his right to a summational categorical description, the usual prerogative of a critical analysis as elegant as Monk's. If his analysis compels him to infer that the sublime does not mark a specific place in literary history so much as a certain power to effect a change in place, he cannot specify this power any more definitively than through a demarcation of the historical realms the sublime disrupts as it passes through.

Under the aegis of the sublime, then, the new found discipline of aesthetics supplanted the rule of rhetoric, and fostered, through its authoritative enchantment, the tastes and styles of what has come to be called the neoclassical period. But having helped form the neoclassical rules of taste, the sublime soon proved too unruly to be included among them. So just as rapidly as rhetoric lost ground to aesthetics, romanticism, armed with its version of the sublime, claimed the territory formerly held by the Augustan age. In this crossover of historical periods, the sublime, in Monk's narrative of usurpation, gathered like an approaching storm all the emotional, political, and psychological elements the neoclassical period found unamenable to its canons. Opposing the orderly, rational, urbane regularity of the Augustan age with the emotional, rude description of the Romantic period, Monk's sublime effected an apparently smooth transition from neoclassical rules to romantic innovations.

But given the demands of Monk's history as Gothic narrative, romanticism as a period and aesthetics as a discipline could not remain the only by-products of this revolution. In transforming the human subject from the role of passive perceiver merely delighting in nature's wonders to the part of dynamic agent awakening to his new found powers as a creator of nature, the sublime installed the genius as the only subject capable of teaching the lessons of aesthetics.

From rhetoric to aesthetics, from the Augustan attitude to the Romantic sensibility, from the creature within to the creator of nature, Monk deploys these elegant narrative transitions as the assurances necessary to compensate for the absence of the promised conclusion to his history, a definitive formulation of the work of the sublime. Able to show what the sublime *does* much more capably than he can define what the sublime *is*, Monk does not evade this duty so much as he claims it is a task already definitively performed. But Monk does not register this claim directly but lodges it in the master transition supervising his entire historical narrative, the movement from the eighteenth century British theoreticians of the sublime to the sublime genius Immanuel Kant, whose work they can only dimly prefigure.

Given his strategic placement of Kant at both the beginning and the end of his history, Monk clearly wishes to put "Kant" to the same use as the "sublime," namely, as a means of delineating and authenticating those otherwise undecidable "turns" in cultural history, the true subject of Monk's narrative. In the economy of Monk's historical representation, Immanuel Kant can define the sublime only because he embodies that genius which the sublime evoked in the romantic subject. As a result of the play of transition in the sublime he embodies, however, Kant makes trouble for Monk's historical scheme even while appearing to corroborate it.

Or perhaps it would be more accurate to say that Kant proved his genius by articulating the trouble at work in those apparently effortless transitions which took the place of a conclusion in Monk's narrative. We can begin to discern the trouble Kant takes in coming to terms with the sublime in his re-examination of the contrast between the beautiful and the sublime which Monk cited as crucial to the formation of the new discipline of aesthetics. Monk of course wishes to collapse this opposition into yet another example of effortless transition, one in which the ideal of beauty in neoclassical art would give way, without any signs of intransigence, to the sublime disruptions of romanticism. Instead of this orderly transition, however, a disturbance occurs at the site of passage. The beautiful does not simply give way but preserves and memoralizes the scenes of sublime devastation. Following the same logic at work in the taste the eighteenth century developed for the ruin, the beautiful memorialized those elements (the tropes of rhetoric, the creaturely in man, and the picturesque in nature) surpassed, or in the terms of the fiction of progress Monk subscribes to, outmoded by the sublime.

Whereas Monk tries and fails to displace the contrast, Kant recovers all the power of that opposition between the beautiful and the sublime by intensifying their differences until they assert themselves with all the force of a contradiction. Curiously, however, Kant refuses to mediate their differences. Instead he exploits this opposition to resolve a contradiction of his own.

Art, according to Kant's memorable maxim, reveals a purposiveness without purpose. In achieving this effect, the beautiful in art takes its lead from the beautiful in nature. Through beauty, nature allows its pure productivity, the sign of genuine freedom, to be enjoyed as an object of nature. But beauty in nature can exert an unwanted effect on the perceiver who, in his dependence on phenomenal objectification, instead of experiencing freedom as his own would always feel compelled to follow nature's lead. Consequently, nature's beauty could deny the freedom it exists to reveal. For, in converting the natural object into an end in itself, the beautiful accrues teleological benefits pure freedom exists to expend. The less beauty depends on an object in nature, the more it resembles the purposelessness "natural" to freedom. In Kant's scheme, art intervenes at precisely the moment when nature needs to be prevented from carrying out her own purposes.

Or to be more accurate, art and nature come to each other's rescue. For subsequent to the intervention of art a curious confusion of roles ensues. When elevated into the realm of pure play characteristic of art, nature is free to assert its independence of the designs of natural law. Paradoxically enough, nature can appear beautiful only insofar as it resembles a work of fine art. But art, on the other hand, must seem to be as free from the constraints of arbitrary rules as if it were spontaneously produced by nature. In this curious turn, Kant engages art and nature in a play of mimesis apparently free of any object to imitate. Art can be beautiful only to the extent that it produces a work as free from artifice as nature, but nature can be beautiful only when it appears as freely imagined as a work of art. Thus nature and art seem to resemble each other less in particulars than in displaced aspirations, as each becomes what the other would like to be. Put otherwise, nature and art become themselves by becoming like the other. But this other each resemble cannot either be the equivalent to or the product of either art or nature but the "independent" power productive of both.

Properly speaking, however, beauty, the delightful manifestation of freedom, applies to their products rather than any productive power giving rise to nature and art. As a secondary formation, beauty cannot reveal this power but only its effects. But consequent to their acknowledgment, these beautiful effects can claim a power formidable enough to demand they be treated as ends in themselves. And in Kant's scheme of things, this demand marks the demise of their freedom. For, by positing an end for art and nature, beauty reinstalls a teleological design, a purposiveness *with* a purpose, art exists to deny.

As if responding to a cue for the *deus ex machina*, the sublime makes its abrupt entrance into Kant's drama in this nick of time, intervening to restore the freedom beauty almost loses. If through beauty, art and nature inevitably manifest a purposiveness freedom orders them to do without, the sublime enables them to meet the demands of freedom by quite literally doing without. Whereas the beautiful glorifies the products of nature and art, the sublime, as a force within nature, utterly extrinisic to natural design, breaks the mold propagating these likenesses. The beautiful domesticates the power productive of art and nature by reducing the locus of its eventuation to the illusion that this power has been exhaustively realized in an object. But the sublime unsettles every locus of power. Not an end in itself but the power to make every end seem preliminary, a sheer force never passing over into specifiable events, the sublime spontaneously surpasses every designation intended to locate it.

In his philosophical drama, then, Kant exploits those

unsettling turns that made so much trouble for Monk's historical narrative. Indeed, in the philosophical equivalent of a recognition scene in a drama, the sublime appears at that moment when nature, in order to be true to Kant's conception of freedom, must produce what produces it. This recognition scene, however, does not resolve so much as it illuminates the contradiction at work in Kant's account of freedom. For in Kant's scenario, it is not nature but the sublime representation of nature which is alone capable of this illumination. In order to achieve this representation, the sublime in nature releases the genius in man who responds to nature as if it were his own creation. In his work of art, the genius draws nature to reflection of its own productive power. "The sublime is an object (of nature) the representation of which determines the mind to think the unattainability of nature as a presentation of nature's ideas." A work of genius, then, redeems the shortcomings of beauty by liberating nature from dependence on any of its beautiful objects and restoring to nature the freedom it produces for itself.

In this dramatic reversal, the sublime turns into the means whereby nature can give its orders to art. As it happens, however, the genius receives these orders as the conflicting commands at once to assert nature's freedom and to assert his independence from nature. Once the sublime aggrandizes Reason at the expense of both Nature and the imaginative apperception of Nature, Kant's drama turns into a rather frightening psychodrama:

> the astonishment which borders on terror; the awe and thrill of devout feeling that takes hold of one . . . is not actual fear, but rather only the attempt to enter into it (fear) with the imagination, in order to feel the power of this faculty in combining with the movement of the mind thereby aroused with its serenity, and of thus being superior to the nature within us, and therefore also to external nature, so far as the latter can have any influence upon our faculty of well-being.

In representing the moment when the Reason recognizes its subservience to the unattainability of nature as a sign of its power over nature, Kant discovers that the sublime dimensions in his philosophy become psychodrama. In this truly astonishing turn of expectations, the Reason, intent on knowing the unattainable expanse of nature, ceases to identify either with the subject or the object of desire but with the blocking agent, the unattainability underlying and intensifying the play of desire itself. Indeed Reason negates both the subject and the object of desire in order to worship an unattainability it, through the act of identification, can claim as its own. In exceeding the bounds of both the subjective ego as well as empirical nature, the Reason can "read" unattainability as the phantom presence of those workings of Reason not yet converted into rational ideas.

Put into the eerier terms its astonishment and fear inspires, in this sublime moment, the Reason witnesses what might be called the spirit of Reason, the effects of Reason independent of any specific rational activity. What generates fear is the dual negation of represented nature and the imagination's power to re-present her. What mollifies fear is another recognition scene: the Reason's identification of this power to displace both Nature and the imagination as its own true work.

In this scene, however, emphasis must be placed on the suddenness rather than the recognition, as the sublime turns out to be the means whereby Reason unintentionally realizes its power. Reason experiences this sudden uplift, this return of power by, if you will, spontaneously laying claim to work it always forgets it has performed. In the economy of Kant's drama of the psyche, the sublime moment spontaneously fulfills Reason's desire to be independent of Nature, without undergoing the trials of either inadequacy or loss. In an instant, compressed enough to require the subreptions of the sublime in order to become comprehensible at all, the Reason experiences an astonishment verging on the brink of fear yet redefines this imminent fear as an enabling power to fulfill the desire for independence even before this desire becomes a conscious wish. Surprised by independence, the Reason initially perceives its own independence as if it were another's, literally independent of it—hence the fear. At the crossroads between astonishment and fear, the imagination redefines fear as astonishment by Reason at Reason's own power—not, however, without reversing the "natural" function of the imagination. Instead of locating the source of the sublime in external nature, the imagination redirects the Reason within when it re-cognizes astonishment as its own negating power. Through the detour of the sublime, then, Reason realizes the fruits of the negative without having had to undergo any specific negation.

As if to suggest it cannot work and be free at the same time, the Reason, in the sublime moment, achieves freedom without having had to undergo a conscious desire for it. And once the imagination provides the Reason with the recognition that not only did it not work but it will not have to work for this freedom, astonishment over the power of independence gives way to serenity over the sense of its achievement. In Kant's sublime economics, then, the fulfillment of Reason's desire for independence spontaneously precedes Reason's awareness of this desire as its own. Consequently, the sublime enables Reason to fulfill its wish as well as to recognize it as its wish in the same instant.

But perhaps we should not depart from this otherwise subliminal recognition of Reason's spontaneous fulfillment of its own purposes without a recognition of our own. As an *unintentional* fulfillment of Reason's purpose, the sublime provides a literal scene for that "purposiveness without purpose," Kant claimed all art existed to realize. Given this transformation of the sublime into a spontaneous fulfillment ironically preceding the consciousness of desire, we might expect Kant to bring the curtain down on this seemingly conclusive moment in his drama of freedom. Resolving the contradiction between nature as freedom and nature as bondage, rescuing beauty from its subservience to objective nature, restituting the exteriority of Reason's to Nature's purposes, if anything the sublime exceeds the philosopher's fondest dream of a triumphant finale for a complicated theoretical system.

Despite our anticipation of his delight,however, Kant does not rest satisfied with the sublime, but must mark it as a place of passage from the aesthetic to the ethical. A moment's reflection on the implications of the sublime for the subject should provide a rationale for this decision. Not an end in itself or even a means to an end, the sublime disrupts the relationship between means and ends that ethics exists to resolve. As if the specular opposite of those wishes the Reason must remain conscious to fulfill, the sublime, as the fulfillment of wishes beyond the fondest dream of reason, makes it necessary for the philosopher to awaken from the sublime if he would recover the integrity of his own reason. The philosopher, if you will, followed his argument to a place supplying it with more force than either the argument or the philosopher deploying it could sustain. If the sublime exempted the Reason from responsibility for the labor of the negative, Kant, as if guilty over having taken so much free time, needs to reclaim responsibility for his work of philosophy. In short, Kant, in compliance with the demands of his argument, must recover ethical responsibility for his argument at the expense of the sublime.

In his theory of the sublime Kant generated a knowledge in excess of the codes of intelligibility meant to constrain experience into a reasonable frame. We might say that the sublime, in locating the place where purpose becomes purposeless, exceeded his philosophic purposes; that is, to provide an ethics as well as an aesthetics of freedom. Unable, from an ethical standpoint, to delight in this excess, Kant re-reads purposelessness as a call back into oneself. For since we never meet purposelessness "outside ourselves, we naturally seek (it) in ourselves, and, in fact, in that which constitutes the ultimate purpose of our being; viz., our moral destination."

Of course, in order to hear this call from within, Kant must literally forget his prior theory of the sublime, for as we have seen, the sublime enables the Reason to encounter its purposive purposelessness as if it originated from outside itself. After having exceeded the given demands of rationality in his theory of the sublime, Kant retreats within an ethical self who treats this excess not as the premature fulfillment of an unarticulated desire, but as the premature articulation of a rational order that is about to be. Or rather Kant identifies the unrepresentable force of this sublime, that presentation beyond representation Kant, in his treatise on the beautiful, suggested both nature and art would like to be, not with anything that already is but with the exemplary deeds the human subject ought to perform. Having in his discourse on the beautiful engaged art and nature in a play of mimesis without any object to imitate, Kant, in his discussion of the sublime does not subvert mimesis but exploits this disturbance in the mimetic process to restore the rule of mimesis. The sublime displaces the object in Nature capable of imitation, condensing it into a process of identification in which the Reason becomes exemplary by imitating itself so forcibly that it becomes what it imitates, which is, according to the logic of the sublime, the representative subject it ought to have been.

In moving from the aesthetic to the ethical, Kant displaces the force of the sublime and treats the code of ethical intelligibility as sublime rather than the experience that is inaccessible to it. After he generates a theory of the sublime that is unassimilable to the constraints of his code of intelligibility, Kant, as if in order to reflect on just this quandary, relocates the trajectory of his critique within the subject. having relocated within the subject, Kant designates the operations of intelligibility rather than the experience "unintelligible" to them as sublime. In other words, Kant utilizes the force of the sublime in order to make the transition from one philosophical category to another seem like the demand for a categorical imperative.

All of this works according to a certain rhythm, Kant wished to translate his discussion of aesthetics of freedom into an ethical framework, but the very subject in aesthetics validating the ethical context simultaneously threatened to disrupt the frame entirely. So Kant made the move to an ethical consideration of freedom concomitant with a displacement of an aesthetics of the sublime, but not without making ethical claims on this disruptive force.

The sublime locates forces not subject to the individual will, and Kant (the locus in Monk's history of the sublime as the figure who recovers moral authority for the individual will), in response both to the threat of these forces as well as the demands of the ethical system he is intent on delineating, compels these to take their orders from his categorical imperative. In the sublime, Kant took up a subject inimical to these patterns and coherences constitutive of our very ability to believe. By impressing the sublime into duty in his overall labor of discovering and authenticating an ethical system, Kant reconsistituted not only an ethical subject he could believe in, but an allegiance to pattern and coherence, the least common denominators of belief itself.

But these observations threaten the elegance of our former assertion. For if earlier we moved from Monk to Kant by remarking on Kant's genius for making trouble for Monk's effortless transitions, we now must pause over a transition Kant wishes to appear if not quite effortless at least purposeless (however ethically purposive this purposelessness may prove to be). Given the terms of our present discussion it would appear that Kant did not prove his genius by becoming the theorist of the sublime but recovered his genius by displacing the topic of the sublime with his true subject, the provenance of ethics. In turning from the sublime to the subject of ethics proper, Kant does not merely turn from one topic to another but turns from a topic unanswerable to the means of differentiating categories to the discipline in which those means (such as coherence and integrity) are identified as moral qualities. And he negotiates this turn as if it constituted his first ethical act. Which is to say that he does not merely turn *from* the sublime but turns to ethics at the precise moment he *needs* to believe in the efficacy of a categorical imperative. And he proves its power. And he proves this efficacy by re-reading the sublime's threat to coherence, unity, and authenticity as a prefiguration of ethical freedom.

This juncture in our discussion provides us with an opportunity to rewrite Monk's history of the sublime. Thus far we have argued that in Kant the sublime disarticulates itself into an instance (of discontinuity) and a force (capable of constraining that disconinuity into a recognizable order). Now let us make one of the assertions this claim endorses. The "history" of the sublime, consequent to an inevitable contamination, produces "history" as an example of the sublime. In this case, history becomes sublime through its power to recover order and authority from the discontinuities threatening them. Should we affiliate order and authority with the process of disciplinization they actualize, we can recognize an "ideal" motive for Kant's disarticulation. The sublime instance as a discontinuity threatening the integrity, unity, and authenticity of any discipline, enables the discipline to demonstrate its authority by eliding this disruption into the continuity of its self-contained operations. The sublime always appears as a threat the various disciplines work their way through to corroborate their claims for authority. We saw, in the case of Kantian ethics, "work" reorients the sublime as a sign of the authority of the discipline.

In the history tracked by Monk, the sublime supervised a double displacement. First, rhetoric was outmoded by the discipline of aesthetics. Then, in Kant, the sublime in aesthetics provided the transition to the interiority of the human subject. Perhaps we can elucidate this "progress" of the sublime by elucidating the rationale for these transitional movements. Eighteenth-century aesthetics displaced the discourse of rhetoric by unmasking its inauthenticity. As an "authentic" inspiration of nature the sublime appeared incompatible with the effects of the rhetorician's tropes. In leading to the rebellion from the rhetorician's discipline to the discourse of aesthetics, the sublime seemed to render every aspect of the "rules" of art synonymous with human freedom. But it did not promote this transfer of power without cost. But in authenticating the sublime at the expense of human work, aesthetics literally required ethics to recover a balance of power. The quest for authenticity oversees each of these transformations. In the final or ethical phase, the human subject "proves" his ethical strength by attributing the disruption to a will become sufficiently sublime to respond in kind.

In this sublime history "unity," "integrity," and "coherence" cease to be merely aesthetic attributes but signs of the ethical labor involved in reclaiming discontinuity as the freedom displayed not *in* but *as* the work of art. In presenting an ideal object whose force was to be at once subdued and contained within the field of aesthetics, the sublime literally provided "moral support" for the newly formulated discipline. The sublime, then, did not appear as one object to be defined along with the others but worked if you will, as the very subject of the new found discipline. For in the field of aesthetics and ethics the sublime actually produces the subjects it appears to disrupt, or rather it enables these subjects as well as the disciplines supporting them to define themselves as an overcoming of sublime disruption.

Of course, as a pure discontinuity, as an abrupt leap, the sublime can also make trouble for the very disciplines it helps to produce. In this context, the sublime can appear as the disruption rather than the "work" of aesthetics or ethics. But disruption constitutes the inspiration for the "work" of both aesthetics (which rereads it as freedom) and ethics (which rereads it as subjective interiority).

In a recent article, the meta-historian Hayden White makes the relationship between this repression of the sublime and the process of disciplinization quite clear. And although White's subject is the relation between the sublime and the invention, in the eighteenth century, of the discipline of history, his remarks apply equally well to the invention of other disciplines.

White tells his story by describing then opposing two different kinds of history, history proper and the inevitably ideological philosophy of history. History proper proves its authority by opposing the philosophy of history with a master narrative that explains all historical events in terms of a utopian design. Instead of supplanting the events of history with the dictates of a master narrative, history proper "tells it like it is." But in a turn virtually returning the critical power of rhetoric, aesthetics and ethics rose to supplant, White claims that this anti-ideological appearance is only disguised ideology, the ideology of the middle as opposed to the high or Longinian mode of rhetoric.

History proper wishes to claim it finds rather than tells its story. But White, in equating both the way of telling and the way of understanding this story with the middle style, discloses the ideological content in this claim. The derhetorization of history proper is only apparent, for such history represses awareness of a rhetoric of the middle style. Buttressed by this rhetoric, the "rules" of historical evidence "overrule" whatever lies outside the middle style, the virtually impregnable realm of taste and common sense. Thus, the apparent process of de-ideologization and de-rhetorization, in making history appear "disciplined," only concealed the ideology at work in historical narrative.

As long as history was subordinated to rhetoric, the "historical field itself . . . had to be viewed as a chaos that made no sense at all but one that could be made to bear as many senses as wit and rhetorical talent could impose upon it." White equates the sublime with this chaos that makes no sense at all. And he argues that history proper represses the sublime by domesticating it with a middle narrative, where taste signifies comprehension, and style is an index of achievement.

In White's meta-narrative, history proper, in its apparent de-rhetorization, does not free its subject from the distortions of political ideology, but only re-affirms a certain type of intelligibility inscribed not within but as the middle style of rhetoric. This mode of intelligibility sets the limits for the rules of the sublime, the means whereby "proper" history recognizes and legitimizes experience. According to this code, properly written histories overrule whatever lies outside the dictates of common sense, taste, and the aesthetically agreeable. Whenever confusion or incoherence threaten proper historical understanding, the narrative of common sense intervenes to constrain extraordinary circumstances into situations consistent enough with the rules of evidence to sound matter of fact. When considered from White's perspective, the taste and style displayed in the writing of "legitimate" history turn out to be epistemological and ethical rather than merely aesthetic categories. As the representation and means of understanding respectively, the middle style turns out to be an index of professional achievement and taste, a sign of authentic comprehension.

In White's view the middle style so refines the explicit appeal to political authority that sublimation, its implicit confirmation of the existent order of things, constitute its mode of political oppression. And this oppression is pervasive enough in the dicipline of history to require a return of the historical sublime, the sheer chaos and moral anarchy of history, as the only means of escape. As long as history is cognizable to the reason plausible to the understanding and interesting to the aesthetic sensibility, it remains deprived of that meaninglessness which alone goads the moral sense of individuals to make their lives different for themselves and their children. Only the return of this experience of sublime confusion can de-sublimate the proprieties formed by legitimate history enough to permit the writing of a visionary history, as the necessary reaction-formation to history's meaninglessness.

Despite its apparent novelty, however, White's narrative of visionary history seems similar enough to our prior narrative of the history of the sublime to be a version of it. But from the perspective of the history of the sublime, it is not the release of the repressed historical sublime that does not constitute the decisive historical event, but the return of the apparently outmoded discipline of rhetoric. On one level, White's meta-narrative of the release of historical sublime from bondage has only been reversed. If we follow White, aesthetics has not surpassed or outmoded rhetoric but only repressed it as the force of every genuine expression.

Moreover, White manages this revaluation of rhetoric by repeating Kant's mode of authenticating aesthetics; that is, through a detour into ethics. Kant, as we saw, invented a theory of aesthetics, in excess of the code of intelligibility meant to constrain experience into its frame. But whenever his theory exceeds the given demands of rationality, Kant retreats within the interiority of the ethical subject, who in his turn experiences this excess as a premature enjoyment of a rational order that is ever more about to be. On retreating to this privileged interiority, however, the ethical subject postulates the mode of intelligibility itself to be sublime rather than the experience inaccessible to it. Consequently, through the sublime Kant can experience the appeal of this mode of intelligibility as the force of a categorical imperative. But whereas Kant claims ethics realizes the freedom art arouses, White maintains that rhetoric, in the excessive arbitrariness of its tropological configurations, activates the confusion and reveals the meaninglessness which is alone capable of inciting the moral will to act differently. But, however much White may wish to claim the rhetorical sublime is not ideological, he has by his own procedure, only converted rhetoric into still another master narrative. If, as White claims, the rhetorical sublime alone can acknowledge the confusion of history by emphasizing the arbitrariness of every effort to make sense of it, White has only used the sublime as a means of authenticating the discipline of rhetoric as a system of tropes even as Kant used the sublime as a means of authenticating the discipline of aesthetics as the display of freedom. But White's meta-narrative proves its mastery by reversing the procedures of Monk and Kant, dismantling their master plots into an exemplary "desublimation" of the progress of history.

Thus rhetoric returns to history the same way it disappeared from it—by means of the sublime. By defining the sublime as a "surpassing" of the arbitrary rules of rhetoric, Monk envisioned the freedom inherent in the newly found subject of aesthetics as the definitive outmoding of rhetoric. By defining the sublime as the recovery of the arbitrariness of rhetoric, White dismantles both the subject of aesthetics and the proprieties of the history it supports. In both instances, the sublime doubles the subject, differentiating it into an ideal other toward which it progresses and an infernal other it regresses to recover. As the exceeding of the bounds of any subject, the sublime does not merely differentiate the subject into its sublimated or desublimated displacement, but by the very force of this displacement, conflates the redoubled subject until it appears to take place as a displacement. The sublime differentiates every subject, and through the displaced subject (whether as discontinuity, force of nature, manifestation of unattainability) differentiation itself exerts all the power of an external authority.

In this oscillation among the disciplines of rhetoric, aesthetics, and history it is in the sublime itself, as if it were the external authority to which each must appeal, that authenticates the various disciplines. When considered from this sublime perspective, rhetoric and aesthetics do not definitively surpass each other as would be the case if the myth of progress inscribing both Monk's history of the sublime and White's latent meta-historical version of the philosophy of history held true. Each at once displaces the other and, in a turn governed by the logic of the return of the repressed, each calls attention to this return of the displaced as well as the process (history defined as the desublimation of the sublime) surpassing this return.

Thus, White's meta-history does not describe but reenacts the process of disciplinization that is seen to have taken root in the eighteenth century's discourse of aesthetics, a process whose power is recognized not as a capacity to define the sublime but to adduce it to its own purposes. But if White defined the integrity of a discipline as its refusal to appeal to external authority, we should now mention what he does not. Such disciplines need not appeal to any external authority. They have co-opted and internalized external authority itself as the work of the sublime.

What remains startlingly fresh in White's treatment arrives from the unregenerated historian in him. For we might say it is Professor White's wish "to tell it like it is" that leads him to equate the utter confusion and chaos of events in history with the sublime. But then we must also say this wish is indistinguishable from the characteristically modern wish to bring history to an end. This may explain the concommitant rise not of modern history but of the related concerns the discipline of history and the discourse of modernism arouse almost simultaneously. It is, after all, an extremely short step from the preoccupation with the definitive narration of what "was" to the confident discrimination of what "is" from what was. But the confidence in this discrimination depends on investing the now with all the force of discontinuity formerly reserved for the sublime.

Modernism reduces the sublime to the shock of the new. For modernism as the wish to tell it like it is separates history, the story of what was, from the force of displacement activating it. In modernism, the force of history, the sheer transition from place to place, distinguishes itself from any controlling pattern whatever. Modernism at once reduces the scale of the myth of progress to the instant, yet prolongs or opens the instant through the "shock" of the new. But this shock can only be experienced as a self-divided wish—to be free of the dead hand of the past yet to experience this freedom as a painful separation from the tradition. Paradoxically, modernism recovers the force of the tradition only in the act of breaking it into instances of the new, and when the multiplication of these instants all contending for control supervenes, modernism defines art as the inability of any of these superogatory orders to make any sense at all.

What results is a world in which differentiation has so totalized the realm of existence that differences have not quite disappeared so much as the possibility of discriminating significant differences has nearly vanished. Modernism's renewed interest in the sublime may constitute an effort to render the pervasive differentiation of the play of modernity significant. For the modernist, the sublime constitutes an effort to translate the anomie and anonymity of the universal play of differentiation into an authentic experience. Modernity, the process of differentiation in which we find elements dislodged from their material, historical, and cultural contexts, uses the sublime to intensify this displacement into a discontinuity radical enough to serve as a locus of authenticity for differentiation itself. The modernist sublime as a force of displacement, intense enough to make displacement appear as if it were an authentic place, as once authorizes change and seems a defense against it. A moment without succession yet the play of temporality itself, the sublime at once takes time yet seems what remains when time passes.

In modernism, the sublime does not move from nature to culture, as was the case in our prior history of the sublime, but from culture to a "neonature" where differentiation, the very mode of being of modern culture, can become itself and be experienced as authentic.

Given White's identification of the historical sublime with the sheer arbitrariness of the rhetorical field, it is not surprising that modernism, as the zero degree of history, should come to terms with its sense of itself as a permanent revolutionary reading its play of displacement in rhetorical terms. This may explain the return from the past of arcane rhetorical terms. "Catachresis," "anacoluthon," "syllepsis," "parabasis," and (a personal favorite) "metalepsis" have all surged up from literature's reserves and been conscripted to contemporary usage. In keeping with their modern usage, however, their return from the past has not resulted in a revaluation of their historical contexts. Instead, all historical contexts as well as the texts forming and formed by them have been assimilated by the infinitely expanding terrain of what has come to be called textuality, a term which provides displacement with sufficient justification to function as its ideology. During this process of assimilation, all the specific differences of both the terms and their contexts have, through the playful rule of *differance*, been effectively read out of them. And consequent to this operation these terms do not seem either renewed or revaluated so much *as subjected to a second outmoding*.

The most recent usage of the term "metalepsis" summarizes this procedure. For metalepsis now describes an ephebe's anxious effort to believe that his work preceded a precursor's. Turned into the differential interplay between *it was* and *not yet*, metalepsis reduces multiple voices from the past to a single voice that pronounces the life-threatening assertion *it was* and settles down the relations between texts by wondering which one will have the privileges of this assertion. Such terms as metalepsis, then, seem to have returned *from* the past only to be returned *to* the past. But they have been returned to the past by an ideology of modernism eager to claim for *itself*, rather than, say, the vicissitudes of literary history, the power to make what was past *seem past*.

Once we discover that these terms return to the past through the neutralizing procedure of "outmoding," however, we can, just as easily, say that these arcane literary terms have truly been made "new." For the "new" works through just such a process of sheer negation. As the "shocking" disruption of an "established" position without positing anything but the distinction from what "has been," the new means this endless procedure of outmoding, it signifies this interminable creation of "has beens." But when we consider that the "new" relegates not only past terms, but, through that ubiquitous preposition "beyond," even the most recent terms to the undefferentiable reserves of outmoded terms, what becomes of the shock of the new? With universal authority but with force, *without force precisely because of the generalization of its operations,* could it be that modernism has returned to these arcane terms from the past to derive power from their archaic rather than their modish strangeness? Is modernism's discontinuity from these arcane terms rendered powerful precisely because they beckon from a past without first having been outmoded?

I want these observations to lead up to these questions. For in their very formulation, these questions recover the force in modernism's renewed interest in the sublime. In harping on the power, strangeness, and discontinuity of the past, these questions do not define the relationship between recent theory and the past as sublime so much as they describe an effort to make that relationship *sound* sublime. The question that now occurs is why does modernism make this effort?

I think we can begin to find an answer to this question when we reflect on the conclusions in the most intelligent recent study of the subject, Thomas Weiskel's *The Romantic Sublime.* In this book the sublime does not evade the trials of outmoding any more than did any of those other terms we mentioned. Unlike Monk's romantic, or Kant's ethical, or White's rhetorical sublime, Weiskel's semiotic sublime does not honor either the "supersensible source" of the sublime power or the human agent who (with increasing success as we move through the history of the term) attempts to usurp this power. Trying to think the sublime in a key different from that provided by the metaphysics of idealism, Weiskel places the sublime in a semiotic context, one in which the relationship between word and thing, sign and referent, man and world, no longer appears *natural* or *given* but arbitrary. In Weiskel's version, the sublime reads what ordinary discourse erases; namely, the felt discontinuity between self and world, sign and referent. Borrowing from Lacanian psychoanalysis, Weiskel *motivates* this erasure by interpreting it as a repression of a frightening experience of alienation, the utter estrangement of words from things a semiotic universe forbodes. Consequent to Weiskel's interpretation, the sublime undergoes a radical change of duty. As was the case with Hayden White, Weiskel does not read the sublime as a power to render the supersensible meaningful. Instead Weiskel reinterprets the supersensible as a repressed recognition of the utterly disorienting arbitrariness concealed within the meaningful. In Weiskel's reading, Reason does not work its way up to a supersensible cognition but, consequent to the sublime appearance of the arbitrariness of its conventional wisdom, Reason works through the loss of its sensible cognitions. If Kant used the sublime as a means of participating in the contradiction between Reason and understanding, semiology uses it as a means of expressing the contradictions between authenticity and differentiation. But in location what makes meaning arbitrary as the source of the sublime, Weiskel has not merely offered one more objective version of the sublime. Instead he has reinvested the anomic energies of the play of *differance*, which as we have suggested is modernism's most recent version of the universal injunction "make it new," with sublime power. By interpreting the sublime as a misrecognition of the power of the new, Weiskel can reread the sublime as a recovery of that shock we earlier found wanting in the new.

As we know, the play of *differance* is no more privileged than any other term. But in elevating the arbitrariness of this play to a sublime plane, a plane, we might add, where idealism found its *historical* justification, hasn't Weiskel if not quite idealized at least secured the sanctions of idealism for the arbitrary? Hasn't the sublime in Weiskel's re-appropriation, but also under such aliases as "the *excess* of signification," the "disruption of the text," the "felt discontinuity between signifier and signified," silently accrued privileges for a mode of modernist thought intent on foreclosing them for everything else? But in light of its levelling effect, its novel proclivity to make differences without the force of distinctions, how else could modernism proceed except through such infusions of power as the modernization of the sublime might provide?

I have suggested that implicitly in its rhetoric and explicitly through a redefinition of the sublime, modernism has used the sublime as a sign of the power of modernism. But having followed the history of the sublime to that modernist movement where history ends in the permament resolution of the sign, I need to end by considering a figure who is answerable neither to that history nor to modernism. I wish now to focus on Emerson, not as an exemplary modern but as a literary figure whose version of the sublime can neither be made new nor historically placed. In terms of our context, he resists modernist appropriation through a version of the sublime answerable neither to idealist nor poststructuralist paradigms, amenable if you will neither to Kant nor to Weiskel.

I do not, however, mean to suggest that Emerson's antinomian use of the sublime can be exhausted by this polarity. In fact I will focus on the Emersonian sublime in order to restore to the discussion what modernism precluded, namely a historical context. More specifically I want to discuss the Emersonian sublime in terms of Emerson's resistance to its ideological use in America and leave implicit the connection between the American sublime and the dogma of the new.

Let's begin with the most famous instance of the sublime in Emerson. Immediately following the "crossing the bare common" sequence and after his transition to the woods, the speaker in "Nature" exclaims "all mean egotism vanishes. I become a transparent eyeball; I am nothing, I see all; the currents of the Universal Being circulate through me." Unlike the Kantian negative sublime defined as Nature's excess of signification simultaneously breaking down the capacity of the understanding and awakening reason as the only agent of comprehension, and unlike the romantic or egotistical sublime arising out of an excess of self, the Emersonian sublime does not elevate either nature or the self to the status of the sublime. Nor, as was the case with the semiotic sublime, does it intensify the sensed arbitrariness in the relationship between self and world. In qualifying the four assertions preceding it, the statement, "the currents of the Universal Being circulate through me," intensifies the sense of transition, the give and take between Nature and the self. In moving from the "transparent eyeball" (more akin to an ear in its power to convert objects into currents of universal Being) to the "me" that forces pass through, the individual crossing the bare common has become less a person than a site of passage, a personification of the confluences between self and nature.

From another perspective, it might be said that in "the transparent eyeball" sequence the speaker unintentionally fulfills the wish imbedded in the question from the introductory paragraph to "Nature," "Why cannot we also enjoy an original relation with Nature?" But this unintentional fulfillment leads to quite an unusual state of affairs. The "transparent eyeball" converts the self who would enjoy Nature and the Nature to be enjoyed into the give and take released by the original question. With neither self nor Nature around to enjoy it, we can only say that the speaker answers the question by himself becoming the original relation between self and nature.

To prevent us from losing either the force of the question or the transformations it evokes, Emerson, as if to signify the ambivalence generated by it, divides the responses elicited by the question into a dialogue between an idealist and a child. The power of this dialogue inheres in the attempt by both parties to totalize the relationship with nature. The child wants utter identification with Nature, the idealist complete independence from it. The idealist wants thoughts without things and the child wants things without thoughts. All the grace and subtlety in the essay derives from the ability of both dialogue partners to maintain the delicate balance of power implicit in their conflicting positions. But the final section, "Idealism," disrupts this balance of power. Here the idealist quite literally arrives at the end of Nature. In converting Nature into his ideas the idealist has brought the natural world to an end. But as soon as the idealist completes his conversion of nature, a voice attributable neither to the idealist nor the child begins to speak: "I do not wish to fling stones at my beautiful mother, nor soil my gentle nest . . . I only wish to indicate the true position of nature in regard to man . . . and bring the mind to call that apparent which it used to call real." The meaning of the extraordinary passage reduces to I do and I do not wish to derealize nature; the propositions are at an equal distance from one another, so that it is impossible to affirm without denying, or the reverse. No sooner do "I" speak from the locus of the child who would not throw stones at his mother than "I" am speaking. Now when as in this passage the "I" who speaks (the idealist) is also an "I" spoken to (by the child), each "I" must be said to speak the discourse of the other. Consequently, the subject of the discourse is always in a displaced position relative to the "I" who is speaking. And a space opens up between what is said and who says it.

While I will return to this scene in a few moments, I want to use this quite literal interruption in Emerson's essay to suggest that it is not only generative of but generated by another discourse carried on in another scene. Behind Emerson's idealist stands an ethos of American liberalism. Moreover this liberal ethos, insisting as it did on man's *in*dependence from nature and tradition, released as a reaction formation to this independence, a frustrated child's need for another world, a world organized around the child's wish for a paradise on earth peopled by noble savages and nature's gentlemen. When we install this Liberal and the child in the dialogue, between idealist and child begun in Emerson's essay, we begin to hear different resonances. Capable dialogue collapses into a vicious double bind. The child's desire to identify with nature leads to the idealist's fear of being engulfed by it. The child's delight in feeling nurtured by nature's bounty leads the independent liberal to force Nature to be bountiful.

In its usage in American religious tracts, political speeches, and landscape paintings the sublime did not call attention to the conflicting demands inherent in liberalism so much as it integrated them to permit a form of double thinking. For in the ideological American rendition, the sublime was not man's but Nature's discourse. And Nature, through rude scenes eloquent with signs of some prior dramatic conflict, some order *beyond Nature*, seemed to command man to get in touch with Nature's higher will and to obey the implicit command to move beyond Nature. Of course the actual source of this will emanated neither from the natural landscape nor from some higher will but from man's future power over the landscape expressed in the policy of western expansionism. Through the subtle turns of the American sublime, the liberal in taking axe and hammer to the virgin land could, with childlike innocence, proclaim that only through destruction of Nature's bounty could he feel by doing what nature commanded as if he were truly in touch with nature's will.

Put simply, the sublime enabled the nineteenth-century American to create a second scene, a veritable world elsewhere where he could rewrite and reread national policies of commercialism and expansionism in quite ideal terms. While in the cultural space opened up by the sublime, the American could impress the feelings of displacement bound to accompany a life centered in the wish to progress, to multiple labors. For example, through a sublime misprision American adventurers and entrepreneurs could reread their alienation from the security of a stable past either as a sign of their exodus from an Old World of habit and custom to a New World of opportunity, or as the success of their revolution against the constraints of their past lives. The difference between their versions would not inhere in the common mythoi of exodus and revolution but in the distinct vehicles for realizing those myths. The frontiersman would treat the everexpanding market fulfill the wish for renewal. But the operating procedure remained the same. Through the dual process of condensation and displacement, the ideology of the sublime turned actual events into rehearsals of those idealized myths of renewal first projected onto nature than read out of her. In fact, the dissemination of the sublime in America, its access to every American rather than merely an aristocratic elite as was the case in Europe, proclaimed the revolutionary democratic character of the sublime sensibility. In the most fundamental sense, the ideology of the sublime constituted and sustained a community of readers who could contemplate the commodification of nature as an elevation of nature into grand ideas. Should anyone happen to feel guilt about this activity, the sublime, through its capacity to instill in the observer the concomitant feelings of diminution and awe, at once punishes the culprit in advance (through the feeling of being dwarfed by Nature) and exonerates him (through feelings of awe and rapture accompanying the vision of the sublime). As "God's ruin" the sublime made the New World seem more ancient than the old; as an expanse of unchartered territory the sublime turned even the most recent settlement into the equivalent of a British stronghold ripe for a rebellious overthrow. Indeed, like the modernist dogma of the new, the American myth of revolution converted into an endlessly repeatable sublime ritual, turned into a tacit form of control.

In his first essay "Nature", Emerson does not condone or corroborate these ideological uses of the sublime. If we digressed from his essay at the point where the discourse between the idealist and the child broke down, we can now see why Emerson let it break down. In Emerson's eyes that dialogue had become bankrupt. Emerson does not follow the national policy of integrating the conflicting demands of idealist and child. Instead he carries their discourse to the point where the *contradiction between* the idealist who wants to master nature and the child who needs to feel mastered by it speaks out with all the pathos of irreconcilability. Implicit in the remark "I do not wish to cast stones at my mother or spoil my gentle nest" is the one question always repressed by the ideology of the sublime. "When we convert Nature's wonders into our commodities how can Nature remain sublime?"

In listening to this other discourse the end of idealism Emerson does not sublimely displace, but lets the mutually destructive import of the dialogue between idealist and child be heard. In Emerson's essay, the idealist does not treat the child's regressive acts of violence as legendary deeds nor does the child convert the idealist's exploitation into signs of union with Nature. Instead, both idealist and child find themselves bereft of nature by the very dialogue they pursue.

But Emerson does not leave them with feelings of bereavment. Neither does he offer a different ideological procedure. Instead he attends to that moment in their dialogue when the idealist and the child bereft of the opposing positions directing their discourse merely face each other with all the openness only total loss can command. If the American sublime converted Nature into a commodity, Emerson dissolved the ideological discourse that sustained this conversion. Separating the idealist from the source of his thoughts and the child from the source of his things, he then has them face each other *before* they can compose their loss into words. Paradoxically, the idealist and the child denuded of everything except the sheer need to respond seem to face each other with an openness denuded of faces. Emerson does not impatiently convert the breakdown in the communication between the idealist and the child into a new line of thought. That would only validate the ideological myths of revolution and progress. Neither does he embarrassedly break the silence speaking between the lines. Instead he abides in the pause, released by this breakdown, that moment in every dialogue when the sheer need to respond overwhelms its every articulation. In this pause, brought into the clear by the confluence of contradiction and bereavement, it is as if the precondition for all discourse, the sheer openness to give and take, were beginning to find words.

When we combine our recognition of a give and take unaccommodable to fixed objectification with Emerson's statement that a material image more or less luminous begins to appear whenever we are thinking aright, we begin to see the transparent eyeball come in appearance *through* this breakdown in the discourse of the idealist and the child. But as we have already seen, the transparent eyeball does not eventuate into an image. Neither a thought nor an image, the transparent eyeball reveals the luminous clearing thoughts and images that pass through to recover their openness. Not a place but the precondition for taking place, or more precisely of letting taking place be, the transparent eyeball, like the pauses in dialogue of the power to make a metaphor, is what every position passes through before it can become itself. The precondition for discourse, signification, and identity, it is what they pass through to become themselves. Yet this clearing appears only when what passes through it disappears. After asking the original question, why cannot we also enjoy an original relation with Nature? with enough force to cause nature and man to disappear, light, the transparent medium of being we never see because we always see through it appears. Put differently, after asking the question why cannot we also enjoy an original relation with Nature which began Emerson's creation of the essay *Nature*, it is as if this question evoked the fiat "let there be light" from another creation of Nature as the only possible response. But since this fiat leads us into a place which is always on the verge of taking place, a place which is neither the infinite play of displacements of modernism nor the mutual surpassing and repressing of forms by history, but makes both possible. That place where returning within and turning toward another become indistinguishable from one another. Put too abruptly, since this fiat leads us to a place which does not take place *in* the sublime but takes the place *of* the sublime, I shall end here.

Chapter 3

On the Border of History: Whitman and the American Sublime

JOSEPH KRONICK

O brilliant kids, frisk with your dog,
Fondle your shell and sticks, bleached
By time and the elements; but there is a line
You must not cross nor even trust beyond it
Spry cordage of your bodies to caresses
Too lichen-faithful from too wide a breast.
The bottom of the sea is cruel.

Hart Crane, "Voyages I"

I will approach Whitman and the sublime in an altogether Whitmanesque fashion—indirectly, but not ahistorically. Thus I begin with Burke's and Kant's concepts of the sublime. First, Burke: "Whatever is fitted in any sort to excite the ideas of pain, and danger, that is to say, whatever is in any sort terrible, or is conversant about terrible objects, or operates in a manner analogous to terror, is a source of the sublime; that is, it is productive of the strongest emotion which the mind is capable of feeling."[1] Burke's notion rests upon a division of the passions into the desire for self-preservation and attachment to society. These two main passions are distinguished by feelings of pain or terror in the former and love of general society and love between the sexes in the latter. Finally, the delight we get from pain is the affective product of the sublime, and the pleasure we derive from an object is the product of the beautiful. The beautiful, at first reading, can be distinguished from the sublime not only by its association with pleasure as opposed to delight, but also in its adhesive quality—it draws society together and helps insure the propagation of the species. But it is sympathy, a passion under the dominion of the sublime, that most firmly binds the individual to society.

By sympathy, "we enter into the concerns of others . . . . For sympathy must be considered as a sort of substitution, by which we are put into the place of another man, and affected in many respects as he is affected . . . ."[2] This passion may turn either pain or pleasure, but it is the bond created by sympathy for the pain of others that is greatest: "as our Creator has designed we shall be united by the bond of sympathy, he has strengthened that bond by a proportionable delight."[3] The delight in relieving the pain of others thus proves to build stronger attachments than does sharing their pleasure, for by relieving the pain of others we relieve our own pain and consequently produce the sensation of delight, which aligns sympathy with the sublime. The greater satisfaction we get out of the sublime passion of delight, as opposed to pleasure in the beautiful, points to a paradox that will have bearing on our consideration of Whitman—the substitution of self for other, by which Burke defines "sympathy," reveals that the sublime isolates the individual from society by the very process that draws him to the other. In relieving the pain of others, man, in fact, primarily aids himself, and the consequent feeling of delight reinforces this isolation as it reveals the gulf separating his feelings from those of others. The Burkean sublime, therefore, produces a sense of isolation as delight in the relief from pain reminds the individual of the unbridgeable chasm between self and other.

Kant's revision of Burke transformed the affective grounds of the beautiful and the sublime from the division of self and society into the division of reason and understanding. The sublime is further divided into the mathematical and the dynamic. The former, which is what I am concerned with, involves the estimation of magnitude and rests in the intuition. To take in an object intuitively through the imagination, the individual must be able to comprehend the object. This, however, would require the logical estimation of magnitude ad infinitum: "Now the proper unchangeable fundamental measure of nature is its absolute whole, which, with it, regarded as a phenomenon, means infinity comprehended." Acknowledging the unrealizable aim of grasping, in total, an endless progression, Kant concludes "that where the size of a natural Object is such that the imagination spends its whole faculty of comprehension upon it is vain, it must carry our concept of nature to a supersensible substrate (underlying both nature and our faculty of thought) which is great beyond every standard of sense. Thus, instead of the object, it is rather the cast of the mind in appreciating it that we have to estimate as *sublime*."[4] Further on, Kant writes, "The feeling of the sublime is, therefore, at once a feeling of displeasure, arising from the inadequacy of imagination in the aesthetic estimation of magnitude to attain to its estimation by reason, and a simultaneously awakened pleasure, arising from this very judgement of the inadequacy of the greatest faculty of sense being in accord with ideas of reason. . . ."[5] The sublime, therefore, resides in the mind of the observer and not in nature. The failure of cognitition in the estimation of magnitude produces simultaneous feelings of pleasure and displeasure which Kant calls the mathematical sublime.

The hierarchical division of mind and nature threatens to be undone in the Kantian sublime, but the assertion of reasons's supremacy over nature, whereby the imagination's failure to grasp infinitude is transformed into a triumphal recognition that this failure has already been anticipated by the laws of reason, thus transports the realm of the sublime from nature to mind and maintains the hierarchy.

While reason serves as the redeeming agent in Kant and instinct serves a similar function in Burke's concept of sympathy, both treatments of the sublime involve a dialectic whereby difference is maintained between self and other, and by virtue of this difference, the self remains inviolable. In Emerson's terms, as Harold Bloom would have it, the sublime is the confrontation of I and the abyss: "There may be two or three or four steps, according to the genius of each, but for every seeing soul there are two absorbing facts,—*I and the Abyss*."[6]

The abyss, as Emerson uses the term, comes from Jacob Boehme and refers to that which existed before the creation. In a journal entry for November 1845, Emerson writes, "There must be the Abyss, Nox, & Chaos out of which all come, & they must never be far off. Cut off the connexion between any of our works & this dread origin & the work is shallow & unsatisfying. That is the strength & excellence of the people, that they lean on this, & the mob is not quite so bad an argument as we are apt to represent it, for it has this divine side."[7] This original abyss, or abysmal origin, has been usurped by the demiurge who has been enthroned as God. Bloom cautions that "language is not the Demiurge, breaking the vessels to a fresh creation of catastrophe. The promulgation of the catastrophe is indeed already the condition of language, the condition of the ruins of time, and of the defense against time, the deep lie at every reimagined origin."[8] Bloom seems to suggest that language itself is the product of the catastrophe; thus the confrontation between I and the Abyss becomes the poet's struggle to reassert his priority over the created world and, in doing so, overcome history.

Bloom's notion of the sublime transforms the confrontation between self and other from the synchronic realm of psychology to the diachronic realm of history and, Bloom would claim, rhetoric. As the demiurge usurps the place of the unnameable and precipitates the Abyss into/upon the Creation, so the poet usurps his ancestors' poems and displaces their work with (and into) his own. The poet who figures most prominently in this scheme is Whitman. Emerson, of course, prepares the ground for Whitman, as well as Bloom's reading of Whitman. In "Experience," he writes that while man is drawn to permanence, "health of body consists in circulation, and sanity of mind in variety or facility of association. We need change of objects."[9] This is as good a source as anything in "The Poet" for Whitman's rhetorical stance as the all-embracing cosmos. And just as Emerson laments the absence of an American bard in "The Poet," so, in "Experience," he laments the lack of expansiveness in man: "There is no power of expansion in men. Our friends early appear to us as representatives of certain ideas which they never pass or exceed. They stand on the brink of the ocean of thought and power, but they never take the single step that would bring them there" (*W*, III:56–57). To produce an art that will endure, one must take this step across the border dividing the I and the abyss. The step across the border into the sea, however, is not a return to origins, but to the chaos that promises forgetting and, hence, renewal. If, as Emerson says, "life is a series of surprises," it is because "God delights to isolate us every day, and hide from us the past and the future. . . . 'You will not remember,' he seems to say, 'and you will not expect' " (*W*, III:67–68). The self preserves itself by virtue of its failure of memory—the inability to recall the past or anticipate the future frees man to live in the present.

Yet, in a less optimistic mood, Emerson would also write, "but every man postpones or remembers; he does not live in the present." (*W*, II:67). In "Self-Reliance," his most famous call for man to free himself from the past, Emerson appeals to origins, here called instinct instead of the abyss: "What is the aboriginal Self, on which a universal reliance may be grounded? . . . The inquiry leads us to that source, at once the essence of genius, of virtue, and of life, which we call Spontaneity or Instinct. We denote this primary wisdom as Intuition, whilst all later teachings are tuitions. In that deep force, the last fact behind which analysis cannot go, all things find their common origin" (*W*, II:63–64). To return to the past and disentangle oneself from the accretions of society and history is to recover intuition:

> And now at last the highest truth of this subject remains unsaid; probably cannot be said; for all that we say is the far-off remembering of the intuition. That thought by what I can now nearest approach to say it, is this. When good is near you, when you have life in yourself, it is not by any known or accustomed way; you shall not discern the footprints of any other; you shall not see the face of man; you shall not hear any name;—the way, the thought, the good, shall be wholly strange and new. It shall exclude example and experience (*W*, II:68).

A re-membered intuition will not be a recovery of man's lost divinity; rather, it will be the dis-covery of a forgotten footprint, a trace. Emerson locates the aboriginal Self in the abyss, the origin before thought, before God and the creation. But can we properly call this Abyss, this Nox and Chaos, an origin? Perhaps, if we follow Bloom and the gnostics. What is Intuition but the moment of blockage, the point which we cannot go if we are not to lose ourselves in the text, that is, in any system of representation, including society and history? The place where analysis cannot go is the region in which the difference between the Me and the Not Me dissolves. But this point of blockage exists only in the remembering, at the limits of language, for it is recognizable only as the "unsaid," as that which resists verbalization; and, as post-Hegelians, we know that negation only affirms what it negates. Intuition, we might say, is precisely that which resists language, and in this very resistance, this blocking of access to origins, we discover not what was merely forgotten, but that language emerges from the abyss called intuition. If "all that we say is a far-off remembering of the intuition," and this intuition remains perpetually new and spontaneous, then language must be the producer of intuition as well as its product. The origin would be already divided, or what today we have learned to call writing—, *differance*.

The search for the aboriginal Self, the Being of man, leads Emerson to the ground, a primary philosophy that man can carry with him. But note that the first philosophy is rooted in the *Abgrund* as much diacritical as monistic, or simply, in a mixture of mixed metaphors:

> The philosophy we want is one of fluxions & mobility; not a house, but a ship in these billows we inhabit. Any angular dogmatic theory would be rent to chips & splinters in this storm of many elements. No, it must be tight & fit to the form of man, to live at all; as a shell is the architecture of a house founded on the sea. . . . The Universe & the individual perpetually act & react on each other. Thus all philosophy begins from Nox & Chaos, the Ground or Abyss which Schelling so celebrates. And in every man we require a bit of night, of chaos, of *Abgrund*, as the spring of a watch turns best on a diamond. In every individual we require a *piece de resistance*, a certain abyss of reliance & fortitude on which to fall back, when worst comes to worst (*JMN*, IX:222–23).

The aboriginal Self will therefore be an abysmal self as well, for the ground of being—and Emerson's equation of ground and abyss translates the pun on *Grund* and *Abgrund*—is accessible only through language, and language, like philosophy of "fluxions & mobility," "is vehicular and transitive, and is good, as ferries and horses are, for conveyance, not as farms and houses are, for homestead" (*W*, III:34). Convenyance, then, is a virtue in both philosophy and language—these two are one for Emerson—because language gives the illusion that man is continually approaching the Universal-Intuition in/as the abyss of being. Universal reliance is grounded on the *Abgrund* (the abyss).

The American sublime does not simply, as Bloom argues, equal the opposition and dialectic of I and the abyss—that is, the poet and tradition; rather, the I is the abyss, and the abyss is language. We can therefore say along with C. S. Peirce that *man* is *language*. But the fear of tumbling back into the abyss, or being swallowed by the past, is not replaced by a merger, fearful or joyful, of Self and Abyss, or what Emerson elsewhere calls the Me and Not Me, for the Abyss inhabits man as that which can never be assimilated with the Self, which, in turn, is unthinkable without the Abyss. The Abyss, language, is that which is uncovered in the past, yet to confront the Abyss is to discover the past as that which lies before man, or is man thought of as always already, in Peirce's terms, a "sign."[10] In Heidegger's words, "An interpretation is never a presuppositionless apprehending of something presented to us. If, when one is engaged in a particular concrete kind of interpretation, in the sense of exact textual interpretation, one likes to appeal [beruft] to what 'stands there,' then one finds what 'stands there' in the first instance is nothing other than the obvious undiscussed assumption [Vormeinung] of the person who does the interpreting." The meaning that is discovered that in the text "has been presented in our forhaving, our fore-sight, and our fore-conception."[11]

In Emerson's terms, the Abyss confronting the I is already possessed by the I in what we call intuition. What we apprehend by intuition is the past, which, for Emerson, is constituted as a text. The aim of the writer is to fill the present with an original reappropriation of language, thus the emphasis on writing and ruins in American literature as interchangeable signs of the fragmentary constitution of the past. The American sublime, therefore, emerges in the recovery of history from the past, and it is as an inscription that history is possessed by the poet. Originality does not mean the creation of a new idea or a new work, nor does it mean the reinterpretation of a precursor's text. To be original is to expose the past that lies before one, and to do so, the poet must cross the border to reappropriate the past and thus meet his own death.

II

Throughout the nineteenth century, history was considered a geological uncovering of successive layers of time that have been reified in language. For the American poet, this meant that his search for originality demanded a return to the ground of language—and this task was frequently undertaken on a literal level that can only be called startling. Hence, we find Whitman conflating English etymology with both cultural and natural history: "The scope of its etymologies is the scope not only of man and civilization, but the history of Nature in all departments, and of the organic Universe, brought up to date; for all are comprehended in words, and their backgrounds."[12] Whitman, who here follows a road mapped out by Emerson in *Nature* and "The Poet," looks at history as a subsidiary discipline of the philosophy of language, even of linguistics (albeit, to call Emerson's, Thoreau's, and Whitman's speculations on language "linguistics" is an abuse of the term). When Whitman says that "the United States inherits by far their most precious possession—the language they talk and write—from the Old World" (*PW*, II:572), he acknowledges that America has no history, that is, a language with which its people may live and think. Whitman's project will be to refashion the language through an etymological uncovering of origins. This presumptive historical task will, however, be conducted on common speech, American slang to be precise, rather than within the Indo-European family of languages. To add authority to his theory, Whitman quotes the English writer John Addington Symonds on language and art as the embodiment of "the nature of the race," the "mythologies" containing the poetic genius of a people. But of those mythologies, writes Symonds, "we are utterly ignorant of their embryology; the true science of Origins is yet in its cradle" (*PW*, II:574). If the science of origins is in its infancy, then we must become further removed from origins before we can recover them. This circuitous path, says Whitman, leads us to the byways of slang, which he defines as "indirection, an attempt of common humanity to escape from bald literalism, and express itself illimitable, which in highest walks produces poets and poems, and doubtless in pre-historic times gave the start to, and perfected, the whole immense tangle of the old mythologies" (*PW*, II:573). Having associated slang with indirection (a turning away from the object) and thus with trope, Whitman then claims that "in the growth of Language it is certain that the retrospect of slang from the start would be the recalling from their nebulous conditions of all that is poetical in the stores of human utterance" (*PW*, II:574). Though not written in slang, this sentence exemplifies indirection. Slang, for Whitman, does not represent a corruption of grammatical speech; it is an original remembering, a retrospect, from the start, of the poetical, which presumably lies both within language and before it in some pre-linguistic stage. Consequently, slang represents an "original" turning away from an origin that cannot be named but only recalled as an unnamable *differance.*

"Slang in America" presents us with an American(?) strategy for dealing with the foreigness of language. Slang serves as a primordial reminder of lost origins and, at the same time, as the vital life of language. Therefore, we can at once study present-day slang as a remnant of origins and as a swerving away from America's European background. Through "circuitous styles of expression" (*PW*, II:574), slang departs from the laws of grammar and returns to an original metaphoricity—thus Whitman's claim that it is in her slang that America will find a native language. Yet all of Whitman's examples represent either borrowed words and place-names or a rather loose syntactical structure featuring numerous circumlocutions.

He ultimately proves unequal to the task of founding an American language, a goal that his analysis undercuts as it progresses. In his eccentric definition of slang as an original retrospection, he suggests that no language is original, for in the beginning was metaphor, a deviation from anything like a proper origin, an original deviation or oxymoron. By thus undermining the concept of originality, Whitman opens a space for himself as an American writer.

Underlying his speculations on language are redefinitions of poetry and history. In his praise for slang, he anticipates Pound's attacks on the subjugation of history and poetry by the monolinear logic of grammer, Williams' rejection of English grammar and syntax as hindrances to an American writing, and Stevens' undoing of a belief in a genealogical descent from a first idea to language. In identifying the poet's dislocation from a native land, and thus, a native tongue, as a displacement from linear history, Whitman redefines history as a poetic interplay between texts. To inscribe America in history, the poet must seek a language that at once differentiates him from his precursors and projects his work into the future. To achieve his ends, he must write a poetics of history, wherein free reign is given to the indeterminable play of metaphor in all human endeavors. Thus we find the predominance of familial metaphors in American literature. A re-creation of the past takes the form of a struggle with literary fathers and a solicitude for future children. Hence, Emerson writes of the need to establish an American literature, and Whitman offers himself as America's bard. Whitman, however, does not present himself as an original, for the poet "shall know that the ground is always ready ploughed and manured . . . others may not know it but he shall. He shall go directly to the creation."[13] The turn to creation is a *re*-turn to the ground, for there language has its origin: "Language, be it remember'd, is not an abstract construction of the learn'd, or of dictionary-makers, but is something arising out of the work, needs, ties, joys, affections, tastes, of long generations of humanity, and has its bases broad and low, close to the ground" (*PW*, II:573). Whitman, apparently, felt more comfortable with the presence of man than did Thoreau, who sought new ground to plow. Both writers, however, follow where Emerson has trod and try to erase his footprints, for the recovery of an American place demands that the past be destroyed. In *Democratic Vistas*, Whitman declares: "I say that democracy can never prove itself beyond cavil, until it founds and luxuriantly grows its own forms of art, poems, schools, theology, *displacing all that exists, or that has been produced anywhere in the past, under opposite influences*" (*PW*, II:365; my emphasis).

III

The task Whitman set for himself in the composition of *Leaves of Grass* seemed to vary with the occasion. In "A Backward Glance," he speaks of it as the record of one man's thoughts and observations. In a note to his executor, Bucke, dated June 1857, Whitman refers to his third edition as "The Great Construction of the New Bible."[14] At other times he describes it as history or even as a type of encyclopedia. But the one thing he continually denied to *Leaves of Grass* was any claim to originality—in the vulgar sense. In his 1855 preface, he embraces the past: "America does not repel the past or what it has produced." (*LG*, 711). Still, for Whitman the past is not present to the poet; it must be dis-covered: "The greatest poet forms the consistence of what is to be from what has been and is. He drags the dead out of their coffins and stands them again on their feet. . . . he says to the past, Rise and walk before me that I may realize you. He learns the lesson. . . . he places himself where the future becomes the present" (*LG*, 718). To make the future present, the poet must resurect the dead, for the future is but the past realized. In making the future a past present, the poet reveals his foreknowledge—that is, what the poet recovers from the past is his future.[15]

The poet's pathway to the present, however, must be through language, and this pathway, says Whitman, proceeds originally by indirection, or diacritically, and not dialectically, no matter his identification of his theory with "Hegelian formulas." In the 1855 Preface, he writes, "the expression of the American poet is to be transcendent and new. It is to be indirect and not direct or descriptive or epic. Its quality goes through these to much more" (*LG*, 714). Although Whitman also writes that the poet "shall go directly to the creation," the pathway has already been broken. The poet's aim is not to find, in the manner of Thoreau, new ground to break, for the scarifier (a tool used to break ground) has left no place unturned, and the compositions of the past have already fertilized the ground. (In "Emerson's books, (The Shadows of Them)," Whitman announces that he "will begin by scarifying "Emerson [*PW*, II:515].) In order to go directly to the creation, the poet must proceed indirectly along the byways of language, for it is in the byways that the "new" is discovered.

Perhaps it was this notion of indirection that made the seaboard so congenial to Whitman. Unlike the ground which bears the traces of his predecessors, the seashore leaves no mark to be directly observed. What Whitman calls the sea, Emerson calls intuition—the place beyond which analysis cannot go. In a section of *Specimen Days* titled "Sea Shore Fancies," Whitman writes, "even as a boy, I had the fancy, the wish, to write a piece, perhaps a poem, about the sea-shore—that suggesting, dividing line, contact, junction, the solid marrying the liquid—that curious, lurking something, (as doubtless every objective form finally becomes to the subjective spirit,) which means far more than its mere first sight, grand as that is—blending the real and ideal, and each made portion of the other" (*PW*, I:138–39). The junction separating sea and land is the unknown, or the Not Me, "that curious, lurking something," which the I can newer comprehend. To assume the power of the poet and step across the boundary separating sea and land is to enter death—thus death as insight. This junction, therefore, joins as much as it separates the objective form and subjective spirit. And it is in death that this simultaneous division and merger occurs. But before we turn to Whitman's poems of sea and death, we need to follow him in the paths of indirection. Having decided that the mystic theme of the sea lay beyond the grasp of "any special lyrical or epical or literary attempt," he declares that "the sea-shore should be an invisible *influence*, a pervading gauge and tally for me, in my composition" (*PW*, I:139). The borderline, the margin we might say, will be Whitman's "gauge and tally," continually inviting him to transgression—that is, to death.

This invitation is heard most distinctly in "Out of the Cradle Endlessly Rocking," which was called "A Word Out of the Sea" in the 1860 edition, and it is this belated edition that I wish to take as my "original" text.[16] In the section once called "Pre-Verse," the poet imagines his return to the past when as a boy he heard a bird's song. But the radical division between the adult speaker and the boy, which is lost in the present participle of the authorized version, is emphasized by the harsh opening line: "Out of the rocked cradle." The past tense marks the division between the poet and his infancy, as the memories invoked by the bird's song turn his thoughts to the past and to death—"the word stronger and more delicious than any." It is this word that leads him back to the scene from his childhood, but it is not a mere child's reminiscence that he sings (which may explain why he dropped the heading from the main body of the poem):

> Throwing myself on the sand, confronting the waves,
> I, chanter of pains and joys, uniter of here and hereafter,
> Taking all hints to use them—but swiftly leaping beyond them,
> A reminiscence sing (*LG 1860*, 270)

The leap beyond the here and hereafter, beyond the waves and back into the past, brings forth a song of death.[17]

In the "Reminiscence," the poet recounts how, as a boy, he heard a bird sing for his lost mate. The bird's song is an invitation transforming the boy into a poet, "the outsetting bard of love":

> Bird! (then said the boy's Soul,)
> Is it indeed toward your mate you sing? or is it mostly to me?
> For I that was a child, my tongue's use sleeping,
> Now that I have heard you,
> Now in a moment I know what I am for—I awake,
> And already a thousand singers—a thousand songs, clearer, louder, more sorrowful than yours,
> A thousand warbling echoes have started to life within me,
> Never to die (*LG 1860*, 275–76).

The bird awakens the soul, which will than go on echoing the song of mourning. In hearing the dirge, the poet realizes the affinity between the soul and death, and thus his tongue is freed to chant a song of death and of himself:

> O throes!
> O you demon, singing by yourself—projecting me,
> O solitary me, listening—never more shall I cease imitating, perpetuating you (*LG 1860*, 276).

As a part of his habit of removing signs of self-doubt, Whitman changed these lines to "O you singer solitary, singing by yourself, projecting me,/O solitary me listening, never more shall I cease perpetuating you" (*LG*, 252). Besides eliminating the obvious hint of the phrase "throes of death," Whitman makes the relationship between himself and the bird more benign as they become sympathetic companions recognizing their mutual solitude. But it is the identification of the bird as his demon, which I take in the older sense of a tutelary spirit, that gives the earlier version more force as it throws doubt on the status of the self, making it a projection of a voice that entices despite (or is it because?) it arouses "the fire, the sweet hell within,/The unknown want, the destiny of me." Whitman will be the poet of unknown desire—that is, of the desire for death:

> O give me some clew!
> O if I am to have so much, let me have more!
> O a word! O what is my destination?
> O I fear it is henceforth chaos!

The child's reminiscence has become a song of destinations, and the return to the past becomes a look into the future, or not quite a vision but an echo, a belated repetition. "The word fixed, superior to all," comes not from the bird that precipitates the poet's reminiscence, but is heard in the perpetual beating of the waves against the shore:

> Are you whispering it, and have been all the time,
> you sea-waves?
> Is that it from your liquid rims and wet sands?
>
> Answering the sea,
> Delaying not, hurrying not,
> Whispered me through the night, and very plainly
> before daybreak,
> Lisped for me constantly the low and delicious word
> DEATH,
> And again Death—ever Death, Death, Death,
> Hissing melodious, neither like the bird, nor like my
> aroused child's heart (*LG 1860*, 277).

In the word from the waves, Whitman hears what Emerson said must reside in the soul of every man—"Chaos, Nox, and the Abyss." (The lure of the sea bears closer resemblance to Freud's concept of the death instinct than it does to his idea of the "oceanic" sense.) To recognize what the child heard in the bird's song, the poet must go forward and possess the premonitions of what lies ahead. The two songs, the bird's and the child's, that he fuses together are a belated construction made possible by another voice—that of the sea. The song of the sea, and thus of death, can only be heard indirectly—as it is echoed in the memory of the song of the bird, for that song leads him to his past and awakens him to death and poetry:

> Which I do not forget,
> But fuse the song of two together,
> That was sung to me in the moonlight on
> Paumanok's gray beach,
> With the thousand responsive songs, at random,
> My own songs, awakened from that hour,
> And with them the key, the word up from the waves,
> The word of the sweetest song, and all songs,
> That strong delicious word which, creeping to my
> feet,
> The sea whispered me (*LG 1860*, 277).

The moment when the poet's songs were awakened is now obscured since it could refer either to the time when he was a child or to the narrative *now* in which he frames the poem. There is even a suggestion that the moment is that of writing, as distinct from the narrative itself, and the songs are yet to be written. This would be particularly appropriate if we agree with Roy Harvey Pearce's suggestion that "A Word Out of the Sea" represents a shift to darker themes in the poems that follow in the 1860 edition.[18] But the word from the sea is not only the word death but the word of the self as well. Although the line, "The sea whispered me," is but Whitman's elliptical phrasing for "The sea whispered *to* me," he nevertheless hints that the sea, in whispering the word "death," also whispers the poet's self, the me myself which is one with death. Death is thus original, not a return to unity but to a marginal or transitional and figural "place."

In a reading of "Song of Myself," Bloom concludes that Whitman transforms the American Sublime from

Emerson's "I and the Abyss" to "*The Abyss of My Self.*"[19] Whitman, says Bloom, so forcefully denies his anteriority that he discovers himself in all he observes and thus forgets his father, Emerson. Bloom's temporal version of the sublime remains within a linear vision of history—the precursor is usurped by his descendants in an entropic process whereby later poets inherit a diminished range of tropes available to them in their war against the past. But poems such as "Out of the Cradle"—as well as "Song of Myself," "As I Ebbed with the Ocean of Life," and "Passage to India"—suggest that language is not born out of a catastrophe that must somehow be denied in the poet's search for the word; instead, the catastrophe lies in the future to be discovered and only belatedly reimagined as precipitating the poem. The catastrophe trope is originary.

In another poem of the seaboard, "As I Ebbed with the Ocean of Life," the poet once again is aroused by the waves to write:

> Elemental drifts!
> O I wish I could impress others as you and the waves
> have just been impressing me (*LG 1860*, 195).

Again I use the 1860 version, since Whitman's changes tend to cover over his skepticism in order to make his poem more cosmic. Thus, he not only eliminates the first two lines and their suggestion of inadequacy, but he also bowdlerizes the following:

> I, musing, late in the autumn day, gazing southward,
> Alone, held by the eternal self of me that threatens
> to get the better of me, and stifle me,
> Was seized by the spirit that trails in the lines under-
> foot,
> In the rim, the sediment, that stands for all the water
> and all the land of the globe (*LG 1860*, 195).

By 1881, the second line becomes, "Held by this electric self out of the pride of which I utter poems" (*LG*, 253). The "eternal self" (the me myself?) that threatens the poet becomes the body electric, the progenitor of children and songs. Whitman eventually recoiled from identifying the transcendent self with "the lines underfoot," which represent not only the ground on which he treads, but also the lines of verse—both his own and his precursors. Once again, Whitman stands in/at the margin, the juncture of sea and shore, and looks at the scraps brought in by the waves as he walks "with that eternal self of me, seeking types."

Typology, the poetry of correspondences, lies on the shores he knows, but as he wends the shores he doesn't know, he hears a dirge:

> I too, but signify, at the utmost, a little washed-up drift,
> A few sands and dead leaves to gather,
> Gather, and merge, myself as part of the sands and drift (*LG 1860*, 196).

The poet is both the drift and its gatherer, and we cannot but think that the dead leaves are his poems. *Leaves of Grass* is a collection without a center, a dissemination of both the poet and his words:

> Aware now, that, amid all the blab whose echoes recoil upon me, I have not once had the least idea who or what I am,
> But that before all my insolent poems the real ME still stands untouched, untold, altogether unreached,
> Withdrawn far, mocking me with mock-congratulatory signs and bows,
> With peals of distant ironical laughter at every word I have written or shall write,
> Striking me with insults till I fall helpless upon the sand (*LG 1860*, 197).

In this touching disavowel of his blithe declaration, "I celebrate myself,/And what I assume you shall assume,"

Whitman turns his back on his pretensions to subsume all mankind and all nature under himself. Collapsed on the sand, the poet submits to nature:

> You oceans both! You tangible land! Nature!
> Be not too rough with me—I submit—I close with
>   you,
> These little shreds still, indeed, stand for all.

This is no metonymic reduction of all poetry to his bardic chant, but rather an admittance that shreds are all that remain of his vision. These lines "stand for all" because all that remains are shreds. Stripped of his illusions, he seeks to restore himself by the agency of the father:

> I throw myself upon your breast, my father,
> I cling to you so that you cannot unloose me,
> I hold you firm, till you answer me something.
>
> Kiss me, my father,
> Touch me with your lips, as I touch those I love,
> Breathe to me, while I hold you alone, the secret of
>   the wondrous murmuring I envy,
> For I fear I shall become crazed, if I cannot emulate
>   it, and utter myself as well as it (*LG 1860*, 198).

To utter the word out of the sea, the word of the father, is to speak oneself. In *The Primer on Words*, he writes, "what a history is folded, folded inward and inward again, in the single word I.—The words of *the Body*!—The words of Parentage! The words of Husband and Wife!—The words of Offspring! The word Mother!—The word Father!"[20] Folded in on the word of myself, the word "I," is the family romance, the struggle of progeny against forebears. The word "I" is the word "history," and yet, it is the word of death. What makes it possible for the poet to write is that he knows time will make space for his lines to lie beside what came before him:

Ebb, ocean of life, (the flow will return,)
Cease not your moaning, you fierce old mother,
Endlessly cry for your castaways—but fear not, deny not me,
Rustle not up so hoarse and angry against my feet, as I touch you, or gather from you.

I mean tenderly by you,
I gather for myself, and for this phantom, looking down where we lead, and following me and mine.

Me and mine!
We, loose winrows, little corpses,
Froth, snowy white, and bubbles,
(See! from my dead lips the ooze exuding at last!
See—the prismatic colors, glistening and rolling!)
Tufts of straw, sands, fragments,
Buoyed hither from many moods, one contradicting another,
From the storm, the long calm, the darkness, the swell,
Musing, pondering, a breath, a briny tear, a dab of liquid or soil,
Up just as much out of fathomless working fermented and thrown,
A limp blossom or two, torn, just as much over waves floating, drifted at random,
Just as much for us that sobbing dirge of Nature,
Just as much, whence we come, that blare of the cloud-trumpets;
We, capricious, brought hither, we know not whence, spread out before you, up there, walking or sitting,
Whoever you are—we too lie in drifts at your feet (*LG 1860*, 198–199).

The eternal self lurking underfoot becomes, in Whitman's reversal, a phantom looking down to discover the corpses, fragments buoyed by the waves and brought to rest as drifts upon the shore. The self lies in the sediment washed upon the beach and thus becomes one with the lines the poet treads upon. The word "death" issued forth from the sea does not silence the poet, for "death is not the ending, as was thought, but rather the real beginning—and that nothing ever is or can be lost, nor ever die, nor soul nor matter" (*PW*, II:420).

Writing marks the absence of the author and therefore frees his work from the Old World formulas of composition. For a New World poetry, a poetry of death, a poetry "consistent with the Hegelian formulas" (*PW*, II:421), and thus a poetry of history, the unfinished work remains to be completed by the reader, and thus the Hegelian future is ever deferred. Having presented himself as the new American poet early in his career, Whitman later laments that America has produced nothing; he therefore describes what it will need in the future: "America demands a poetry that is bold, modern, and all-surrounding and kosmical, as she is herself. It must in no respect ignore science or the modern, but inspire itself with science and the modern. It must bend its vision toward the future, more than the past" (*PW*, II:412). A return to the ground is not enough; there must be a way to think this ground, and this way leads through the book, hence the emphasis on the role of the reader from Emerson to the moderns.

In an 1883 article, "The Bible as Poetry," Whitman states, "No really great song can ever attain full purport till long after the death of its singer—till it has accrued and incorporated the many passions, many joys and sorrows, it has itself arous'd" (*PW*, II:548). If the song is to incorporate the responses it has elicited, it must possess these responses in advance as a forhaving, a prepossession that will only be realized in the response of the reader. The text incorporates as the other what it already possesses unknown to itself. The American book, says Whitman in *Democratic Vistas*, will proceed by indirection, and "the reader is to do something himself, must be on the alert, must himself or herself construct indeed the poem, argument, history, metaphysical essay—the text furnishing the hints, the clue, the start or frame-work. Not the book needs so much to be the complete thing, but the reader of the book does" (*PW*, II:425). The text, by necessity, must be incomplete if it is to be a reflection of America, which is also incomplete. Whitman's "service . . . must be to break a sort of first path or track, no matter how rude and ungeometrical" (*PW*, II:393). With his poems of hints, America's first poetry becomes "trace" as "origin."

Whitman's characterization of his work as furnishing hints to later writers and readers is not an act of modesty—after all, he was little given a modesty. The founding of a new literature for America must be a recovery of America's past from its European origins. Whitman will discover America's future history in the text of the past and of nature. But this text must be set in a new type, if not a new language:

> Not only is the human and artificial world we have establish'd in the West a radical departure from anything hitherto known—not only men and politics, and all that goes with them—but Nature itself, in the main sense, its construction, is different. The same old font of type, of course, but set up to a text never composed or issued before. For Nature consists not only in itself, objectively, but at least just as much in its subjective reflection from the person, spirit, age, looking at it, in the midst of it, and absorbing it—faithfully sends back the characteristic beliefs of the time or individual—takes, and readily gives again, the physiognomy of any nation or literature—falls like a great elastic veil on a face, or like the molding plaster on a statue (*PW*, II:484-85).

Rather than require a new language, America will need to readapt language to a new set of circumstances, or in Whitman's metaphor, reset the type to a text which has not yet come into existence. Before this text will be issued, Nature must be read into existence, much like the poem must be completed by the reader. America, the "inheritor of the past, is the custodian of the future of humanity" (*PW*, II:513), but America, and that means democracy, has not yet come into being; its history, like Nature's, "remains unwritten, because that history has yet to be enacted" (*PW*, II:393). The problem facing the American writer is that he will drape nature in a veil or an inherited vision of the world. Thus, to enact a history for America, the poet must displace his precursors and clear the way for his writings.

Yet, as we have previously observed, Whitman's notion of displacement does not entail a claim for originality. In a note apparently intended to be used by a friend who was writing an article on *Leaves of Grass*, he writes: "Walt Whitman's philosophy—or perhaps metaphysics, to give it a more definite name—as evinced in his poems, and running through them and sometimes quite palpable in his verses, but far oftener latent, and like the unseen roots or sap of trees—is not the least of his peculiarities—one must not say originalities, for Whitman himself disdains originality—at least in the superficial sense. His notion explicitly is that there is nothing new only an accumulation or fruitage or carrying out these new occasions and requirements" (*CW*, IX:12).

The poet's work will be one of indirection. To quote again from the 1855 Preface: "the expression of the American poet is to be transcendent and new. It is to be indirect and not direct or descriptive or epic. Its qualities goes through these to much more" (*LG*, 714). Whitman rejects rhyme, meter, and ornamentation not only because he associates them with the outmoded art of the Old World, but also for their uselessness in an age of print and writing.[21] Writing is the body of language. Thus in "Starting from Paumanok" (originally "Proto-Leaf"), he compares the body to printer's type:

> Of your real body and any man's or woman's real
> body,
> Item for item it will elude the hands of the corpse-

cleaners and pass to fitting spheres,
Carrying what has accrued to it from the moment of birth to the moment of death.

Not the types set up by the printer return their impression, the meaning, the main concern,
Any more than a man's substance and life or a woman's substance and life return in the body and the soul,
Indifferently before death and after death.

Behold, the body includes and is the meaning, the main concern, and includes and is the soul;
Whoever you are, how superb and how divine is your body, or any part of it! (*LG*, 23–24).

Like the text which gathers into itself the readers' experiences, the body carries all that it has accrued. And like the printer's type, which disseminates meaning through the impressions made from it, the substance of life inheres in the book of the body—before and after death. Hence readers who seek an original voice are mere corpse-cleaners washing the text of its diacritical marks. The communicability of meaning beyond death makes meaning possible. Whitman's insistence on the body as text and text as body (we should recall the famous line, "Comerado, this is no book/Who touches this touches a man" *LG*, 505) stands outside the tradition so thoroughly analyzed by Derrida according to which the effacement of the signifier guarantees the existence of truth.[22] For Whitman—and this is what makes indirection so important a concept in his poetry—truth is always derivative; it is inextricably bound to history in a process whereby the signified is only knowable in its reconstitution in the trace, hence his emphasis on the need of every reader to reconstruct the book. Without a fixed notion of the self—and his Me Myself, real Me, and I all suggest the dissolution of the unified self—there is no voice to attach to the text. And his fascination and dread of the earth, "the compost of billions of premature corpses" (*LG*, 209), reflects his recognition that life is generated by death. Finally, his fear ultimately rests on the linkage between death and writing—he must possess death in order to write. His words are the compost that will fertilize America—"If you want me again look for me under your bootsoles" (*LG*, 89).

Later in life, Whitman could not refer to his discovery of the ties between death and writing with such buoyancy. His most explicit treatment of death and writing may be found in "Passage to India." In the 1876 Preface to the centennial edition, he has a long footnote in which he reevaluates his life's work in terms of his more recent compositions. In a parenthetical remark within the note, he writes, "then probably 'Passage to India,' and its cluster, are but freer vent and fuller expression to what, from the first, and so on throughout, more or less lurks in my writings, underneath every page, every line, everywhere" (*PW*, II:465). He presents "Passage to India" as an "emblem of rest and aspiration after action—of crown and point which all lives and poems should steadily have reference to, namely, the justified and noble termination of our identity, this grade of it, and outlet-preparation to another grade" (*PW*, II:467). While Whitman was never so unorthodox in his religious beliefs as to deny the existence of an afterlife, his characterization of it became more conventional in his later years. But his embrace of the past does not represent a departure from his 1855 preface. Nevertheless, the opening of the poem is striking in its mixture of declamation and metaphysics:

> Singing my days,
> Singing the great achievements of the present,
> Singing the strong light works of engineers,
> Our modern wonders, (the antique ponderous Seven
> outvied,)
> In the Old World the east the Suez canal,
> The New by its mighty railroad spann'd,
> The seas inlaid with eloquent gentle wires;

Yet first to sound, and ever sound, the cry with thee
O soul,
The Past! The Past! The Past!

The Past—the dark unfathom'd retrospect!
The teeming gulf—the sleepers and the shadows!
The past—the infinite greatness of the past!
For what is the present after all but a growth out of
the past?
(As a projectile from'd, impell'd, passing a certain
line, so still keeps on,
So the present utterly form'd, impell'd by the past.)
(*LG*, 411–12).

Whitman will return later in the poem to this conflation of man's technical triumph over geography with the overcoming of time, and hint of a past beyond time, beyond retrospection. In a note he writes, "We know of no beginning in the universal literature, any more than in chronology. We only [know] what is first to be mentioned" (*CW*, IX:105). Unlike Melville, then, Whitman seems to rest easily with his disavowal of origins. His notion of an "unfathomed retrospect" hints of the inaccessible nature of what lies outside representation. Nor does he think of the present as an organic growth, as his question suggests. The final lines posit the present as already existing fully formed in the past; therefore, to direct one's vision toward the past is but to try and see the present. This would seem to violate Emerson's injunction that we live in the present, but Whitman's remembering is not a postponement, only a discovery of what one must already possess.

His passage to India is a journey, at once to the past and the present, but it is also a journey that leads him into the future:

Passage to India!
Lo, soul, seest thou no God's purpose from the first?
The earth to be spann'd, connected by network,

The races, neighbors, to marry and be given in marriage,
The oceans to be cross'd, the distant brought near,
The lands to be welded together (*LG*, 412).

Whitman here repeats the commonplace nineteenth-century notion that a geographical linking of the world represents both a physical merger of the continents and a merger of the ancient world with the modern. (This, by the way, is one of the key ideas in Michelet's *Introduction a l'histoire universelle*. Whitman could have easily picked up this idea from Arnold Guyot's *Earth and Man*, a work combining geography with political and social history.[23])

Whitman sees in man's technological feats a fulfillment of Columbus' dream:

The plans, the voyages again, the expeditions;
Again Vasco de Gama sails forth,
Again the knowledge gain'd, the mariner's compass,
Lands found and nations born, thou born America,
For purpose vast, man's long probation fill'd,
Thou rondure of the world at last accomplish'd. (*LG*, 414).

In circumnavigating the world, man has found a passage to the past and thus, in fulfilling his probation, brings forth the present. And in completing the voyage, Whitman asserts himself as the poet who will complete the work of scientists and therfore prove himself "the true son of God." The poet will recover from the past its secret and restore the harmony of man and nature. The "retrospect brought forward" and the vision of history are characterized as a return to Eden:

Passage indeed O soul to primal thought,
Not lands and seas alone, thy own clear freshness,
The young maturity of brood and bloom,
To realms of budding bibles.

O soul, repressless, I with thee and thou with me,
Thy circumnavigation of the world begin,
Of man, the voyage of his mind's return,
To reason's early paradise,
Back, back to wisdom's birth, to innocent intuitions,
Again with fair creation (*LG*, 418).

The return to "man's early paradise" will be a joining of East and West, a return to an earliness not touched by history. Whitman's prophetic voyage takes him back to what Emerson, who was of a tougher fiber than Whitman, called the abyss. The crossing of the border—actually, a circumnavigation of the globe—will mean the mastery of death:

Passage to you, your shores, ye aged enigmas!
Passage to you, to mastership of you, ye strangling
  problems!
You, strew'd with the wrecks of skeletons, that,
  living, never reach'd you (*LG*, 420).

"Passage to India" may be Whitman's most programmatic effort at writing a poem consistent with modern science, at least his eccentric version of it, for the poet's vision is a fulfillment of the scientist's work. Technology will be the instrument of the soul's voyage to "primal thought." The soul's return is not a recovery of a lost innocence, but the discovery of the future. Eden, says Whitman, is what lies before us.

In the Whitmanean version of an American sublime, the step across the border—the margin that keeps his text afloat amidst a sea of texts—will bring the poet before that "primal thought" Emerson called Instinct. To recover a claim to originality, Whitman hopes to travel "back to wisdom's birth, to innocent intuitions," but he was too good a student of Emerson to ever believe that an originary intuition could be innocent (we might say that his tuition came at too high a price). A Passage to India is a retrospect—and thus a repetition—of the Emersonian confrontation of I and the abyss, the diacritical space of writing. And the scene of writing is "strew'd with the wrecks of skeletons," the texts of poets who violated the margins demarcating the I and the abyss in order to dis-cover language once again in the traces of a sublime always already inscribed in/as the figure of an "originary" deviation Whitman variously identifies as death, the sea, and writing.

Notes

1. Edmund Burke, *A philosophical Enquiry into the Origin of Our Ideas of the Sublime and Beautiful*, edited by J. T. Boulton (1958; rpt. Notre Dame, Indiana: University of Notre Dame Press, 1968), 39.

2. Ibid., 44.

3. Ibid., 46.

4. Immanuel Kant, *The Critique of Judgement*, translated by James Creed Meredith (Oxford: Clarendon Press, 1952), 104.

5. Ibid., 106.

6. Stephen E. Whicher (ed.), *Selections from Ralph Waldo Emerson* (Boston: Houghton Mifflin, 1957), 405.

7. Ralph Waldo Emerson, *Journals and Miscellaneous Notebooks*, edited by William H. Gilman, et al. (Cambridge: Harvard University Press, 1960–), IX, 325. Hereafter cited as *JMN*.

8. Harold Bloom, "Agon: Revisionism and Critical Personality," *Raritan* 1; 1 (Summer 1981), 31.

9. Ralph Waldo Emerson, *Complete Works*, centenary edition, edited by E. W. Emerson (Boston: Houghton Mifflin, 1903–4), III, 55. Hereafter cited as *W*.

10. See C. S. Peirce's "Some Consequences of Four Incapacities": "It is sufficient to say that there is no element whatever of man's consciousness which has not something cor-

responding to it in the word; and the reason is obvious. It is that the word or sign which man uses *is* the man himself. For, as the fact that every thought is a sign, taken in conjunction with the fact that life is a train of thought, proves that man is a sign; so, that every thought is an *external* sign, proves that man is an external sign." *Philosophical Writings of Peirce*, edited by Justus Buchler, originally published as *The Philosophy of Peirce: Selected Writings* (1940: rpt. New York: Dover Publications, 1955), 249. In a forthcoming essay, "Emerson and the 'American' Signature," Joseph N. Riddel undertakes a detailed study of Peirce's theory of the sign and its relationship to Emerson's speculations on language and nature.

11. Martin Heidegger, *Being and Time*, translated by John Macquarrie and Edward Robinson (New York: Harper & Row, 1962), 191–92.

12. Walt Whitman, *Prose Works 1892: Specimen Days, Collect and Other Prose*, edited by Floyd Stovall (New York: New York University Press, 1963), II; 572. Hereafter cited as *PW*.

13. Walt Whitman, *Leaves of Grass: Comprehensive Readers Edition*, edited by Harold W. Blodgett and Sculley Bradley (New York: W. W. Norton, 1965), 717. Citations from the 1855 preface and from the poetry, unless otherwise indicated, are from this edition. Hereafter cited as *LG*.

14. Walt Whitman, *The Complete Writings*, edited by Richard Maurice Bucke, et al. (New York: Putnam's, 1902), IX; 6. Hereafter cited as *CW*.

15. For a rigorous Heideggerean reading of Whitman and the recollection of the past, see Paul Bové's important essay in *Destructive Poetics: Heidegger and Modern American Poetry* (New York: Columbia University Press, 1980), 131–79.

16. Walt Whitman, *Leaves of Grass: Facsimile Edition of 1860 Text*, introduction by Roy Harvey Pearce (Ithaca: Cornell University Press, 1961). Pearce's introduction provides a strong case for the superior quality of the early versions of several of the major poems. His argument that this is Whitman's best book is also important. This text will hereafter be cited as *LG 1860*.

18. *LG 1860*, xl.

19. Harold Bloom, *Poetry and Repression: Revisionism from Blake to Stevens* (New Haven: Yale University Press, 1976), 266.

20. Walt Whitman, *Daybooks and Notebooks*, edited by William White (New York: New York University Press, 1978), III; 733.

21. See *CW*; IX:36: "The origination and continuance of metre, and of rhyme afterwards, were not only from their pleasantness to the barbaric ear, but more from their convenience to the memory in arresting and retaining tales and recitations and passing along what they tell from person to person, generation after generation, preserving the epic song or ballad ages and ages as was often done in old times without the aid of writing or print."

22. See Jacques Derrida, *Of Grammatology*, translated by Gayatri Chakravorty Spivak (Baltimore: Johns Hopkins University Press, 1976).

23. Arnold Guyot, *The Earth and Man: Lectures on Comparative Geography in Its Relation to the History of Mankind*, translated by C. C. Felton (Boston: Gould and Lincoln, 1855).

Chapter 4

Dickinson and the Haunting of the Self

HELEN REGUEIRO ELAM

One would expect the experience of the sublime to make possible for the poet a moment of wholeness—a moment in which the self is at one with itself, at one with the world it has created or envisaged. Yet this expectation of sublimity is consistently thwarted in post-Enlightenment poetry, and the sublime appears instead as an experience of doubling and negativity—an abysmal experience of self-loss. In *Paradise Lost*, well before the fall, Adam feels his solitude encroaching upon him, and in response he is given "Thy likeness, thy fit help, thy other self,/Thy wish exactly to thy heart's desire" (VIII, 450–51). Eve is, in God's reading of her, Adam's other self and thus the wholeness for which he yearns. But Milton's reading suggests not only that the "original" self of Adam is already haunted by poverty and dearth, but that the very being constituted to bring about his wholeness is already troubled by its own doubling. Eve sees herself and loves herself before she comes to love Adam. Adam's "other self," an image of a consciousness that seeks to become whole by assimilating the otherness which it constitutes, is already beset by the otherness it attempts to heal. At the center of Eden, as well as in Adam's mind, is unveiled the abyss.

Dickinson is haunted by this otherness which poetry tries to heal and which it reveals. There are Emersonian moments in her poetry in which she seeks for herself the perfect coincidence which she witnesses in nature. Yet the moments of sublimity occur not when she contemplates the in-itselfness of nature, but when she sees within herself that breach between self and soul, between consciousness and identity, which Emerson called the abyss. Milton's request of the muse—"What in me is dark/Illumin"—is granted in Dickinson with a vengeance, for the dark is for her indeed illuminated, but without it ever being displaced by the light. Over and over again Dickinson sings because she must, "to keep the dark away," yet the singing is already a vision into absence, a seeing of the dark which she tries to displace.

At times Dickinson seeks for herself, in Emersonian fashion, the perfect coincidence which she witnesses in nature. "There is a Zone whose even Years" pointedly yearns for this moment in which consciousness is no longer displacement but the condition of fulfilment:

> There is a Zone whose even Years
> No Solstice interrupt—
> Whose Sun constructs perpetual Noon
> Whose perfect Seasons wait—
>
> Whose Summer set in Summer, till
> The Centuries of June
> And Centuries of August cease
> And Consciousness—is Noon. (1056)[1]

Human time appears absent from the poem, and even natural time—the movement of the seasons—is arrested in a moment of perpetual noon. The high point of the sun, without solstice, without morning or afternoon, is sustained in the "evenness" of this magical "zone." And the season becomes absolute—set in itself—as if nature here rejected temporality and made the centuries "cease." The poem envisages a moment of arrested peace, where years and centuries come to a halt in this impossible coincidence of sun and self. The consciousness that is noon must also, necessarily, be the consciousness that "constructs" that noon, the consciousness that cannot conceive of otherness or of an outside that opposes itself to consciousness' interiority.[2]

The existence of this zone or of this moment is predicated on the absence of any "interruption," yet interruption characterizes the Dickinsonian universe, both in the potential relation between self and nature and in the most intimate relation of consciousness with itself. Indeed, the first becomes a metaphor for the second, for when Dickinson speaks of intimacy with nature she is positing a vision of wholeness in which consciousness and identity would sustain rather than "hound" each other. The breach in consciousness appears first as a breach between consciousness and nature, and is translated into the impossibility of "overtaking" the retreating horizon:

A Light exists in Spring
Not present on the Year
At any other period—
When March is scarcely here

A Color stands abroad
On solitary Fields
That Science cannot overtake
But Human Nature feels.

It waits upon the Lawn,
It shows the furthest Tree
Upon the furthest Slope you know
It almost speaks to you.

Then as Horizons step
Or Noons report away
Without the Formula of sound
It passes and we stay—

A quality of loss
Affecting our Content
As Trade had suddenly encroached
Upon a Sacrament. (812)

The poem creates a series of thresholds which it cannot cross, and the impossibility of crossing is already a translation of consciousness' inability to contruct perpetual noon. The light in Dickinson is always a tenuous and tentative occurrence, surprising the self with its apparition, and with its disparition abandoning the self to its own dark. The first line of the poem posits the light in rather precise terms (a light exists in Spring), but the rest of the poem places that light beyond the range of certain apprehension. The light exists when March is "scarcely" here, at the "furthest" slope, and "almost" speaks to the poet. Not quite there, yet making its presence felt as an imminent revelation, the light propels the poem into a space where it might cross over and "overtake" the object it so tenuously posits. The light "waits" in the landscape, it reveals ("shows") the natural objects, and it is there so insistently that it almost acquires a voice. But the poem traces the possibility of crossings that do not occur, and the potential voice of nature is translated into an otherness that interrupts the poem's impetus even as it gives it voice.[3]

The last two stanzas witness the passing—the displacement—of the light, and the poem's reaction to the disappearance of its subject. Emerson tells us that we have learned of the horizon the art of perpetual retreating and reference. The Emersonian horizon is first of all a limit which the self must transgress. But it also functions in Emerson as a mobile reference point from which the self appears to retreat and be displaced. The horizon in Emerson affirms both centrality and the impossibility of centrality. In the Dickinson poem, it is nature that silently and stealthily passes out of the reach of the poet's voice. Horizons and noons—the limits of the horizontal and vertical ranges of vision—"step" and "report away/Without the Formula of sound," and the poem names that absence "encroachment," as if instead of "overtaking" nature it had instead been overtaken by its absence. The light that "almost speaks" reports away without reporting, without voicing its passage, and its silence is the poem's trope for its own absence, for the dark within itself that the poem comes to see. Nothing marks the passage of the light except the "passage" which is the poem itself, so that the poem voices here its own silence, the otherness which traverses it and which it cannot name. The sacrament at the end is the impossible sacrament of self-coincidence; and the poem is inevitably the encroaching trade, which encroaches not so much on nature as on the possibilities of its own voicing. The poem's trade in the sense of a metaphysical exchange encroaches on a sacrament that can only be apprehended through that trade, so that the poem here witnesses its own absence, its "internal difference" from itself. What it apprehends, finally, is its own otherness, its "quality of loss," out of which it both speaks and reports away.

The internal difference that breaches the poem figures centrally in "There's a certain Slant of light":

There's a certain Slant of light,
Winter Afternoons—
That oppresses, like the Heft
Of Cathedral Tunes—

Heavenly Hurt, it gives us—
We can find no scar,
But internal difference,
Where the Meanings, are—

None may teach it—Any—
'Tis the Seal Despair—
An imperial affliction
Sent us of the Air—

When it comes, the Landscape listens—
Shadows—hold their breath—
When it goes, 'tis like the Distance
On the look of Death— (258)

The light, as in the preceding poem, appears and disappears in nature, but the poem's subject is the self's response to its passage. The light of Winter, like the light of Spring, is a trope for the poem's "difference" from itself which its "trade" cannot heal. Its presence leaves no trace, no scar, but it reveals to the poem the "internal difference" of its own meanings, that is to say, the poem's inability to fully utter itself. The poem cannot "read" itself, gather itself together ("None may teach it—Any—"). It can only read itself as difference, as absence from itself.

The slant of light, like the light that exists in Spring, changes everything in and by its passage. But so does the poem. At its presence, landscape and shadows "hold their breath," as if awaiting precisely not its presence but its disparition. And its passing opens an empty, unfocused space— "like the Distance/On the look of Death"—the space from which the poem speaks and in which it is trapped. The "passing" of light and poem is thus double-edged, for "passage" bespeaks both presence and disappearance, and what the poem witnesses is the "mark" of its own difference, of its own passage through itself. It traverses its own otherness, and "seals" itself in the space of its own impossibility. If Dickinson's poems appear to come from a strange unidentifiable space, this is because the process of voicing is simultaneously for her a process of discovering the empty space from which that voice emerges. The slant of light and poetic voice are airy nothings—sent us of the air—but they are also the imperial affliction that invisibly "scars" or breaches the poem's will to fullness. The poem that witnesses its own passage afflicts itself with the knowledge of its own abyss, and "seals" itself in this in-between space of consciousness from which it simultaneously sings to keep the dark away and reveals the dark the light traverses.

Otherness is thus the central experience of the Dickinsonian universe, for nature eludes the poet's attempted possession, and consciousness cannot construct a privileged, self-fulfilling space that is not breached by the knowledge of its own dark. The proleptic vision of oneness in "There is a Zone" is repeatedly breached in the major Dickinsonian texts that deal with consciousness and poetic creation, for those texts create a strange literary space in which both the integrity of consciousness and the possibility of poetic voice are put into question—in which the self is haunted by the knowledge of its own abyss, and poetry made more difficult by that knowledge.

"I felt a Funeral, in my Brain" attempts to voice the abyss that threatens the self, and the ritual of the funeral offers a comforting, enclosing, circumscribed space for the self to fit into. To engage in ritual is to exclude the more frightening possibilities of absence, and Dickinson starts out with the prospect of a controlled vision of the abyss. By the end of the first stanza, sense breaking through appears to sustain the possibility of an ordered universe in which reason—sense—triumphs over vacancy.

> I felt a Funeral, in my Brain,
> And Mourners to and fro
> Kept treading—treading—till it seemed
> That Sense was breaking through—
>
> And when they were all seated,
> A Service, like a Drum—
> Kept beating—beating—till I thought
> My Mind was going numb—
>
> And then I heard them lift a Box
> And creak across my Soul
> With those same Boots of Lead, again,
> Then Space—began to toll,
>
> As all the Heavens were a Bell,
> And Being, but an Ear,
> And I, and Silence, some strange Race
> Wrecked, solitary, here—
>
> And then a Plank in Reason, broke,
> and I dropped down, and down—
> And hit a World, at every plunge,
> And Finished knowing—then— (280)

The second stanza repeats the notion of ritual of the first—the service for the dead—but the repetition of the single sound here, like the treading of the mourners to and fro in the first stanza, suggests that repetition is not controlled by ritual. On the contrary, repetition haunts the mind, as if the funeral were not the ritual after the fact of death but the cause of the event it is supposed to ritualize. The funeral thus reveals itself to be a funeral of the imagination, and the poem an account of the process by which poetic vision breaks down. The poem begins with the poet hearing the sounds of the funeral—coming to "sense" as hearing—but the fourth stanza places her outside the range of hearing and outside the possibility of being. When space tolls, the heavens are a bell and being but an ear, but the poet is beyond sensory recognition or imaginative redemption. Aligned with silence, wrecked as a poet even before a plank in reason breaks, she speaks of the impossibility of poetic speech, and silence becomes a strange metonymy for the poem's recognition of its own death. The poet ends in the fourth stanza "wrecked, solitary, here—" but the "here" refers to a space that cannot be defined in relation to the opening of the poem. As in "Because I could not stop for Death" or "Our journey had advanced," the last two stanzas of this poem place the speaker in a space in which she knows but cannot utter that knowledge, a space in which poetic metaphor cannot encompass the vision of horror which the poem has unveiled.[4]

Thus "I felt a Funeral, in my Brain" traces the breakdown of poetic voice, and ends with a vision of the abyss that cannot be uttered by the very voice that has opened it up. Sense—in the sense of reason—appears to break through in the first stanza, and the funeral provides the meaning entrenched in ritual. But the last stanza escapes the comforting round of ritual, and the plank of reason—the flimsy structure that holds sense together—breaks down to reveal the abyss. This is, perhaps, the point at which sense finally breaks through into the poetic world, but its breaking through is also a breaking under, for the poet falls into an endless space, and "finishes knowing" that which the poem cannot utter. The "then" suggests that the poem starts over again, compulsively repeating the motions that lead up to the final recognition in which the speaker is trapped. This is, perhaps, what Dickinson means in another poem when she says that she "could not see to see." The seeing is a voicing, but poetry breaks under the weight of the vision it is supposed to sustain. We reach in this poem an aporia in which we cannot define or contain the content of the poet's vision, but in which we can recognize the sublimity of her encounter—her attempted utterance of that which she does not wish to see or know. "I am on the brink of frightful speech," says the herdsman to Oedipus. "And I of frightful hearing," replies Oedipus, "yet I must hear." The Dickinsonian universe does not make possible the triumph of knowledge central to classical tragedy, and this makes her act of peering into the violent abyss all the more sublime. She transgresses, in the Kantian sense, the boundaries that constitute identity, but without ever achieving what Kant describes as the point at which a supersensible reason derives pleasure from the experience which produced imaginative terror. The terror in Dickinson is always present, and sublimity resides in her repeated seeing of the abyss.

Seeing in Dickinson is a metaphor for voicing, and to "see" the abyss is at the same time to find herself in an undefinable, unspeakable space and to voice that very "unvoiceability." If her poems appear the most dense and contradictory in the language, it is because they "rest" on and are "wrested" from the space in which silence and voice are caught in a narcissistic doubling of each other, almost as if the self were voicing its own silence, its own abysmal depths. "I saw no Way" builds on this identification of silence and voice, and makes it impossible to locate the origin of the poem. The poem seems to stem from an impasse of interpretation, and repeatedly converges upon that impasse, reopening the space of impossibility:

> I saw no Way—The Heavens were stitched—
> I felt the Columns close—
> The Earth reversed her Hemispheres—
> I touched the Universe—
>
> And back it slid—and I alone—
> A Speck upon a Ball—
> Went out upon Circumference—
> Beyond the Dip of Bell— (378)

The proleptic vision of oneness of "There is a Zone" is exactly reversed hère, and becomes prolepsis of a consciousness that can never be "noon" because its vision is a vision of entrapment and dissolution. The poet begins by seeing no way, and the end of the poem leaves her beyond the prospect of vision. The first stanza witnesses the closing and enclosing universe. Though stitching is a kind of mending, the mending here is deadly, for it closes the poet in and forecloses the "way." In the second line, no longer seeing, she "felt" the columns close—that is, come close together and emphasize the stitching that allows no seeing through. The third line, however, offers a sudden upheaval, for the world overturns and thus the question of vision is reopened. Yet the poet is not said to "see" in the rest of the poem. She "touches" the universe, and "it" slides back and leaves her sliding in turn into an open and deadly space, into a circumference that cannot be measured or voiced. It is as if the heavens in the second stanza were unstitched, as if their "breaking" were the condition of her voicing. The reversal of the earth's hemispheres in the first stanza suggests the reopening of what was closed to the poet, but what the poem opens up into is a vision of the void. Even the term "vision" is catachresis here, for the poet "feels" and "touches" and finally ceases mentioning the senses, as if the sliding and the slipping were apprehended through some internal sense of imbalance—an infinite fall into or out to a space "beyond."[5] The poem's possibility of "seeing" falters here, for it reaches once again the impasse of its own silence, and speaks from within its depths. In the first line the poet *sees* that there is no way. In the last line, as in "I felt a Funeral," she is beyond touch and beyond hearing as well, "out upon" circumference, but this circumference retraces the opening steps—the way she cannot see. The poem paradoxically voices the vision of its own silence, endlessly repeating its "seeing" into nothing, into its own abyss.

"The Loneliness One dare not sound," more powerfully than the preceding poem, unveils this abyss which threatens the poet with its revelation:

> The Loneliness One dare not sound—
> And would as soon surmise
> As in its Grave go plumbing
> To ascertain the size—
>
> The Loneliness whose worst alarm
> Is lest itself should see—
> And perish from before itself
> For just a scrutiny—
>
> The Horror not to be surveyed—
> But skirted in the Dark—
> With Consciousness suspended—
> And Being under Lock—
>
> I fear me this—is Loneliness—
> The Maker of the soul
> It's Caverns and it's Corridors
> Illuminate—or seal— (777)

The poem organizes itself around tropes of measurement—sounding, plumbing, surveying—and its impulse is to avoid measuring the self for fear that it may reveal itself to be boundless. Yet the process of writing the poem is, paradoxically, such a measurement. Loneliness (which Hartman translates as "oneliness")[6] lies at the origin of the poem,and the writing of the poem is at the same time the "sounding" which the poem attempts to circumvent.

The first stanza describes loneliness by a metaphor that consciously falls short of its subject, so that loneliness appears more abysmal than the grave, more far-reaching than death. Critics systematically comment on the centrality of death in Dickinson's poetry, but death in Dickinson is only a metaphor for a loneliness so profound that the self risks disappearing in the face of that recognition. This is why in the second stanza the self fears that moment of vision—the moment in which it can see its own depths. To see itself is to perish from before itself, to disappear in the face of its own vacancy. The abyss for Dickinson lies always within, and the fear is that the poet's resources will not be strong enough to counter the vision that poetry reveals.

Because the poem appears to move in two opposite directions—toward concealment or repression and toward illumination—it brings about a disjunction between theme and rhetorical event that is never quite mastered. The third stanza again attempts to turn away from the vision of vacancy, to keep consciousness suspended and being under lock. But consciousness is not suspended, being is not under lock. Rhetorically the poem sounds, plumbs, surveys, and the power of its rhetoric lies in the fact that the metaphors of binding space reveal that space to be boundless, and reveal the speaker trapped in that moment of recognition. The poem thus does not swerve away from but aligns itself with consciousness and loneliness, and the horror—the "chasm" in one manuscript version—which it finally witnesses at the same time gives it voice and threatens it with dissolution.

This disjunction between theme and rhetoric is brought into focus by the "this" of the last stanza. Grammatically, the poem's three subordinate clauses move toward this point in which the main subject is uttered, and in the utterance is a concentration of all that the poem purported to avoid. Grammar and rhetoric combine here to give the last stanza the weight of revelation. "I fear me this—is Loneliness—" unveils the horror which the poem up to now has forestalled, and pinpoints the moment of crisis—the moment in which loneliness is identified as the maker of the soul:

> I fear me this—is Loneliness—
> The Maker of the soul
> It's Caverns and it's Corridors
> Illuminate—or seal—

As in "I felt a Funeral, in my Brain," the speaker here comes to a recognition of where she has always been—trapped in a space which she cannot encircle. The poem traces not the process of her entrapment, but the process of her recognition. By the end of the poem she is no further than she was in the beginning, but as in "I felt a Funeral" she ends up "knowing"—a knowledge which simultaneously makes and breaks the poem. The poem originates in this moment of seeing and surveying the possibilities of its own dissolution, and as it illuminates the chasm from which it emerges it "seals" the soul in the vision of its own identity. One is tempted at first to read the "maker of the soul" as some deity external to the poem who illuminates or seals the caverns and corridors of the soul. But the rhetorical impetus of the poem, and the grammatical disjunction between presumed subject and verb in the last stanza, force a reading that identifies Loneliness with the Maker of the soul: the caverns and corridors of the soul illuminate or seal loneliness, which is the maker. There is no maker in this poem other than loneliness, and what it makes (the poem) is haunted by this knowledge. The poem represses (seals) this knowledge, but in sealing also illuminates it. The "or" in the last line is misleading, for the poem reveals illumination to be also a sealing in, a repeated and inevitable recognition by the soul that its origins lie in its own loneliness, which is to say in its own abyss. Dickinson's poems do not assimilate and control the otherness which haunts them. But they do put into evidence the problems that arise out of this inability at self-origination. The confrontation with that otherness makes possible a moment of simultaneous disruption and sublimity—a moment in which, like Stevens, she sees into the violent abyss and voices the very silence that threatens her, a moment in which the voicing is already the seeing into the abyss.

Over and over again Dickinson's poems uncover this abyss within the self. In "This Consciousness that is aware" the soul at first appears to be self-sufficient, adequate unto itself, yet that adequacy turns to self-haunting by the end of the poem and the poet is left once again trapped in a consciousness whose vision she cannot choose to ignore:

> This consciousness that is aware
> Of Neighbors and the Sun
> Will be the one aware of Death
> And that itself alone
>
> Is traversing the interval
> Experience between
> And most profound experiment
> Appointed unto Men—
>
> How adequate unto itself
> It's properties shall be
> Itself unto itself and none
> Shall make discovery.
>
> Adventure most unto itself
> The Soul condemned to be—
> Attended by a single Hound
> It's own identity. (822)

Dickinson's poetry encompasses a whole universe with ease. Neighbors, the sun, and death are synecdoches for all human experience, and she suggests that the consciousness which can take in neighbors and the sun—the human and the natural—can also comprehend ("be aware of") death. Death, in other words, is here assimilated into consciousness, for the fact of awareness is itself a traversing of the "interval" between experience and death and thus makes death an "experiment," one more experience in life. Consciousness here lays claim to a plenitude which rivals God's, and sees itself as its own "maker," as if the writing of the poem were already the traversing by which consciousness becomes absolute.[7]

Indeed, in the third stanza consciousness underscores this absoluteness, its adequacy unto itself. Yet that moment of achieved adequacy is itself ambiguous, for as in "the Loneliness One dare not sound" we are forced to read the first two stanzas backwards in order to make grammatical sense of them. Dickinson's use of dashes in this poem is sparse, but the grammatical difficulty between stanzas one and two puts into question the vision of plenitude which the poem proffers. The poem's affirmation of its adequacy is undermined here and in the third stanza, for the interval between experience and most profound experiment is revealed as an interval *in* the self, an interruption in which consciousness sees itself and sees its own abyss.

The third stanza prepares for this revelation because it presents the soul's adequacy as its exclusivity, its self-enclosure—the movement by which it shuts itself off from what is not itself. Once again in this poem the soul selects her own society and shuts the door, and the presumed assimilation of neighbors, the sun, and death into itself is not a strong enough distraction to turn it away from self-scrutiny. These are not "properties" of the soul, and thus they are displaced in the poem's impetus toward self-recognition.

As the soul discovers itself it closes itself from others' discovery ("Itself unto itself and none/Shall make discovery"), and the ultimate self-assertion is also the ultimate isolation. The quest for self-sufficiency and self-origination entail, necessarily, this final self-enclosure. The soul at the end of the poem is condemned to be adventure most unto itself, which is to say that it must be subject and object of its experiences, sealed in by its own will to adequacy. The consciousness that is aware of nature and death must ultimately be aware of itself, and this means to be hounded by itself—to see, as in "The Loneliness One dare not sound," its own abyss. All other subjects of the poem—neighbors, the sun, and death—disappear in the presence of the soul's vision of itself, for the soul takes them in and then takes itself in—sees itself in the interval of its own making as "wrecked, solitary, here." The soul's experience of itself in this poem (adventure most unto itself) is the ultimate and most devastating experiment (most profound experiment) it can enter into, and one which it is unable to master. Consciousness here hounds—hunts—haunts the poetic self, and like "I felt a Funeral," "The Loneliness One dare not sound," "I saw no Way," the poem appears to break under the strain of its revelation. Indeed, it is this breaking that constitutes its voicing, for the breaking sustains that Dickinsonian intimacy between voicing and silence. Dickinson's poems are haunted by this simultaneity of voicing and silence, that is to say, by their own impossibility. The sublime for her is always a negative moment, a moment of crisis in which the voicing is a "seeing" into the dark—a triumph over the darkness that threatens to engulf it, but also an unveiling of the very silence out of which it constitutes itself. The "being" of the poem lies in its very otherness, and its power in its ability to "illumine" its own dark.

Notes

1. All quotations are from *The Poems of Emily Dickinson*, edited by Thomas H. Johnson. 3 vols. (Cambridge, Mass., The Belknap Press of Harvard University Press, 1955.

2. Joanne Feit Diehl sees "the poet's ability to render stasis at will" in this poem (*Dickinson and the Romantic Imagination* [Princeton, N.J.: Princeton University Press, 1981], 90.). Sharon Cameron, on the other hand, reads temporal disjunction in the poem ("Summer will last . . . only 'till . . . August cease' "). (*Lyric Time: Dickinson and the Limits of Genre* [Baltimore: Johns Hopkins University Press, 1979], 139).

3. For an excellent discussion of this poem in terms of language-as-loss, see Cameron, 181–182.

4. David Porter refers to these as "poems of the aftermath" (*Dickinson: The Modern Idiom* [Cambridge, Mass.: Harvard University Press, 1981] 10).

5. Cameron rightly speaks of a "language . . . giddy with the speaker's disorientation" in this poem (*Lyric Time*, 9).

6. Geoffrey H. Hartman, *Criticism in the Wilderness* (New Haven: Yale University Press, 1980), 126.

7. For readings of the poem that take death as a trope for consciousness, see Robert Weisbuch, *Emily Dickinson's Poetry* (Chicago: University of Chicago Press, 1972), 83, and Harold Bloom, *Figures of Capable Imagination* (New York: The Seabury Press, 1976), 94.

Chapter 5

Emily Dickinson's Calculated Sublime

GARY LEE STONUM

1. Sublimity and Power

Roughly two hundred of Emily Dickinson's poems include some reference to mathematical terms and ideas.[1] Although hardly the most conspicuous feature of her poetry, it is a highly unusual one for her time. Indeed, in an age of poets who generally shared Goethe's scorn for mathematics, Dickinson's practice is genuinely idiosyncratic, as much so as her punctuation or syntax. On the other hand, Dickinson's calculations operate squarely within this otherwise antimathematical literary tradition. She counts and measures in order to address a central concern or romanticism, the challenge of the sublime. More specifically, mathematics serves Dickinson as a strategy in the poetics of power.

In a general way, Dickinson's poetry undoubtedly courts the romantic sublime. Her work is everywhere manifestly concerned with transcendent experience, and it is fired by an extraordinarily intense, bold poetic ambition. To her sister-in-law, for example, Dickinson wrote the following: "Cherish Power—dear— Remember that stands in the Bible between the Kingdom and the Glory, because it is wilder than either of them."[2] Despite the playfulness of Dickinson's tone, the advice is seriously meant, and it aptly summarizes a recognizable and widely held poetic ambition. Power, wildness, and a share in divine exaltation are essential attributes of the sublime; the first two are particularly endorsed, under one name or another, by nearly all the diverse accounts of sublimity produced in the eighteenth and nineteenth centuries.[3] Dickinson's understanding of the sublime may be most emphatically revealed by another letter written by her late in life. Jacob's wrestling with the angel is one of the touchstones, even the cliches, of scriptural sublimity; in the letter; Dickinson refers directly to this passage, calling Jacob "Pugilist and Poet" and praising his audacity. Her identification of poetry as a sublime contest of strength is clear enough, but the astonishing thing about the letter is that she misquotes Genesis. Her Jacob says to the angel, "I will not let thee go, except *I* bless *thee*" (my italics).[4] As a sublime, combative poet, in other words, Jacob reserves even the power of blessing to himself.

Nominating Dickinson as a poet of the sublime may be slightly premature, however. Unlike the poets who expressly sought to achieve sublimity (and in so doing, like Wordsworth, may have significantly revised our understanding of the notion), Dickinson is always more interested in power as such. The difference between power and sublimity as poetic goals can probably never be great; certainly Dickinson's pursuit of power leads her through several familiar topoi of the sublime. Nevertheless, placing her work under the rubric of power makes for a slightly different focus. It guards against prejudging a crucial issue in her work: the relation between external forces and those she claims as her own.

Power is a word Dickinson rarely fails to capitalize; it belongs with presence, circumference, and a few others as one of the central animating abstractions in her poetry. Sometimes indistinguishable from the state she calls "bliss," to her power chiefly means the capacity to command awe. In addition to the word itself, her chief terms for power are the privileges of royal rank—palaces, dominions, crowns, and the like—and marital union with the potent suitor who normally carries an aura of the sacred. These tropes unite in the figure of queenhood, her most frequent image for the state of power.

In addition to what she claims to exert of herself, Dickinson experiences power as emanating from three sometimes related sources: the quasi-sacred lover or suitor; nature in its most glorious, self-sufficient, and hence alien aspect; and a divinity who usually resembles the first person of the Christian trinity.[5] From any and all of these sources power both entices and assaults. It entices by promising to bestow itself upon her, and it assaults by threatening to overwhelm her selfhood and her native capacities.

This combination of allure and selfhood is characteristic of the sublime, which always begins as the fascination of painful, excessive, or terrifying experiences. As the earlier eighteenth-century practice of cataloging the objects of sublime experience gave way to a more subjective esthetics, the main issue in speculations on the sublime became the one Kant first resolved convincingly: how does the mind convert an initial terror and confusion, which check or rebuke its capacities, into the psychic exaltation that we are pleased to call transcendence? With certain changes of emphasis, notably stemming from psychoanalytic ideas, this remains the key question in modern theories of the sublime.[6]

The prejudice of the sublime, if I may so rashly characterize a fairly diverse body of thought, is for some form of identification as the answer to this question. The orthodox sublime is initiated by an external object that seems to dwarf the mind, and it is concluded by a reaffirmation or enlargement of the mind's powers. The mind is thus usually understood to have identified with an hence appropriated the force of what had been or seemed external.

Identificatory theories of the sublime chiefly vary according to how they view the object. In its simplest form, identification proceeds according to what must be the most frequently quoted passage in Longinus. "Our soul is uplifted by the true sublime; it takes a proud flight, and is filled with joy and vaunting, *as though it has itself produced what it has heard*" (my italics, but also those of many earlier commentators).[7] This is a reader's or beholder's sublime, one that emphasizes the authentic majesty of the object. Longinus's conception of that majesty is clear from his praise of conflict in the *Iliad.*

According to most accounts influenced by Freud, the object is less a power in itself than a symbol of forces arising from primal fantasies. Identification with such forces normally resembles what Freud himself meant by the term; the process parallels or recapitulates an oedipal struggle (superimposed perhaps on preoedipal fantasies of devouring and being devoured).[8] Crudely put, a man dispels the threat of castration by identifying himself with the father's phallic power. This can variously involve having overcome, become, or become one with the father.

In Kant's analytic, the object merely occasions a purely psychic drama; identification occurs entirely within the orbit of the mind. This might seem to preclude what Longinus and the Freudians stress, a dependence on superior forces outside the self, but to the initially balked imagination an identification with reasons' triumphant powers must also seem like submission to something external. Reason's advent, Kant insists, is the curiously bracing discovery that one is subject to a universal law. The invigoration in this discovery presumably comes from the mind's identification with a faculty of its own. This requires, however, the chastening and then the obeisance of other faculties. In addition, despite the stipulated universality of reason, Kant explicitly distinguishes the sublime access to reason's kingdom from what is properly feminine. His example is the enobling experience of civilized warfare.[9]

Two themes should be clear from this obviously

tendentious survey: the identification with an alien power and the persistent masculinizing of the struggle with that power. Dickinson objects to both themes. As feminists have recently argued, Dickinson has some necessary reservations about man-to-man combat; she at least understands the struggle according to different gender rules.[10] Dickinson also shares a more fundamental objection with the most antinomian strain of American literature. Simply put, this is the prideful insistence on one's own powers, and a concomitant rejection of external forces. Whitman issues the characteristic American boast in *Song of Myself*!

> Dazzling and tremendous how quick the sunrise
> would kill me,
> If I could not now and always send sun-rise out of
> me.

Such strength depends on externality only to the degree that it is a reactive counterpower; in other respects it is thoroughly unsponsored. Although Dickinson is often less blithely confident about the efficacy of her powers (so, frequently, is Whitman), her most exuberant proclamation of native omnipotence asks whether even God can match such might:

> To be alive—is Power-
> Existence—in itself—
> Without a further function—
> Omnipotence—Enough—
>
> To be alive—and Will!
> 'Tis able as a God—
> The Maker—of Ourselves—be what—
> Such being Finitude! (no. 677)[11]

There has yet to be a poet who maintained such claims thoroughly and consistently. Indeed, the boastful lines from

Song of Myself introduce a sequence in which Whitman is overwhelmed by the sensations of hearing and touch. In "Out of the Cradle Endlessly Rocking" he undergoes a more typical instance of the romantic sublime: helpless grief leads to identification with an external power and instigates the birth of the poetic career. Dickinson, too, will sometimes characterize power as the outcome of taming anguish. In "I can wade grief" (no. 252) she says that "Power is only Pain/Stranded, thro' Discipline." On the other hand, if I accurately construe the puzzling line ("Till Weights—will hang—") that follows this memorable aphorism, disciplined power is only a temporary recourse. It allows the self to withstand a sudden shock, but only until balance is restored and the self again commands its native resources. Moreover, discipline implies a controlled and deliberate response to pain. It would thus seem to exclude the involuntary self-abandonment that normally precipitates sublime identification.

Even the poems in which external power most strongly tempts or threatens typically stage a deliberate hesitation at the edge of transcendence. Cognizant of the reputed or promised benefits but reluctant to surrender herself, Dickinson always insists on her prerogative of choosing freely. "I'm ceded—I've stopped being Their's—" (no. 508), for example, compares the involuntary baptism suffered by the child to the willed choice of crown, queenhood, and supremest name. The final stanza emphasizes the strength and autonomy of that willing and the correspondingly greater majesty of what she elects:

> My second Rank—too small the first—
> Crowned—Crowing—on my Father's breast—
> A half unconscious Queen—
> But this time—Adequate—Erect,
> And with Will to choose, or to reject,
> And I choose, just a Crown—

Yet if she has indeed stopped being theirs, if she is no

longer in thrall to a series of masters that begins with her father, includes the ministers of the church, and culminates perhaps in a heavenly father, she is still nonetheless ceded. Power and rank lie elsewhere, in the gift of some less definable agency. Gaining them requires that she submit, albeit deliberately.

Poem 508 articluates the central dilemma in Dickinson's poetry: the conflict between internal freedom and external power. On the whole, Dickinson is about as extreme a poet as our country has produced in the strength of her resistance to alien power. Her use of mathematics as a native counterpower, furthermore, is nearly unique among American poets. However, one prerequisite of the mathematical strategy clearly affiliates her with the mainstream of American romanticism.

Dickinson learned a great deal from Emerson, and one of her larger debts arises from his having partly freed the idea of power from the conceptual grasp of epistemology. In saying that Dickinson experiences power as emanating from several objects (and from herself), I have meant to equivocate about whether it is a property of these sources. Emerson's influence on her seems to have assisted Dickinson's instinct for divorcing psychic states from the objects that instigate them or are said to embody them.

Overlaid on the subject-object dichotomies of Lockean thought and also on the division of mental faculties stressed by Kant and Coleridge, Emerson's theater of the sublime consists of three largely autonomous actors. Freedom, Fate, and Power are their most general names.[12] Freedom—also known as solitude and whim—is largely the conscious will and sometimes the whole of *Nature*'s me, but Emerson typically emphasizes its capriciousness. We thus cannot unguardedly take it as the poet's ego or character. Fate, which in Emerson's canon begins as nature and ends as society, is largely the objective, material world, but it includes at least the temperamental aspects of selfhood that "Experience" describes. The crucial distinction is that Power (alias genius, the central man, the giant, and so forth) is not a property of fate but an influx that is independent of any concrete course or occasion. Likewise, in spite of the anthropomorphic nicknames, power does not reliably belong to freedom.

The separation of power from fate affords Dickinson an enormous advantage. It partly frees the desired potency from the dialectical double binds of subject and object or self and other, and hence from the specular abyss to which they so readily lead. (Think, for example, of Shelley's *Alastor.*) On the other hand, the cost of Emerson's triad, visible throughout nineteenth-century American literature and much of that of twentieth-, is that power becomes a rather ghostly phenomenon. No longer surely exercised by the heroic figures who make themselves a fate in the world and not even quite a property of awesome natural forces, power comes to be understood as an oddly intransitive state of being, like the greatness of Jay Gatsby.[13] This dematerialization of power goes hand in hand with the American vision of an imperial self, a mind that can blithely transcend the gritty realities manifested in a generalissimo or a dynamo.

2. Ratios and Sums

Mathematics can serve as one form of the defensive discipline invoked in "I can wade grief." Algebra, for example, defends against the agonies encountered in poem 269:

> Bound—a trouble—
> And lives can bear it!
> Limit—how deep a bleeding go!
> So—many—drops of vital scarlet—
> Deal with the soul
> As with Algebra!
>
> Tell it the Ages—to a cypher—
> And it will ache—contented—on—
> Sing—at it's pain—as any Workman—
> Notching the fall of the Even Sun!

The first stanza's especially compressed syntax allows it to be read alternately as a cry of desperation and of exultation. The former reading appeals for some boundary to agony, one that would preserve the calm rationality needed for algebraic computation. The latter exclaims that algebra erects just such a boundary and can therefore defend the soul's integrity. Bleeding does not confound algebra, only the algebraist. Thus the second stanza advises that calibrated accounts can make life bearable, as any laborer knows when he counts the hours until quitting time and as any poet knows when she sings the fall of what had seemed a just and kindly natural world.

Counting the ages of pain down to zero makes for a notably dim glory, however, one that belongs more to stoic consolation than sublime heroics. Elsewhere, mathematics is more directly enlisted in the sublime combat between freedom and power. In "A solemn thing—it was—I said—" (no. 271) the temptation is to drop one's life into the mystic well and so to wear the white blameless mystery of a bride of God. The first three stanzas ponder the bliss that such submission would afford:

> And then—the size of this "small" life—
> The Sages—call it small—
> Swelled—like Horizons—in my breast
> And I sneered—softly—"small"!

The speaker's rejection of holy sacrifice can be understood to provide a skeptical gloss on "just" in the otherwise imperious "And I choose, just a Crown." The rejection is made possible by the modest computational skill of measurement, specifically the comparison of life's finite horizon-filling size to the plummetless dimensions of eternity. ("Plummetless," otherwise an elegant trope for infinity, also functions quite literally to mean that which cannot be accurately plumbed.) The important thing is that, aside from her life, mathematical skill is the only resource in the poem that is the speaker's own.

Comparing life with afterlife, time with eternity, and

earth with heaven is a pervasive strategy in Dickinson's poetry. Robert Weisbuch has identified the practice as a form of typology, the scrutiny of earthly moments as prefigurations of what lies beyond.[14] The typological order itself is beyond Dickinson's control, but the calculation of type against antetype is not. Such calculation produces what poem 88 calls a ratio:

> As by the dead we love to sit
> Become so wondrous dear—
> As for the lost we grapple
> Tho' all the rest are here—
>
> In broken mathematics
> We estimate our prize
> Vast—in it's fading ratio
> To our penurious eyes!

All three Emersonian agencies are at least nominally present in this brief lyric: Fate in the form of death and loss, Power in the form of the prize we intend to claim, and Freedom first in the act of estimating and second in the penurious eyes, selves that the adjective precisely names as both impoverished and stingy, at once longing for the prize and unwilling to invest life to gain it.

Ratio, the geometric quotient of two quantities, is one of the two crucial mathematical ideas in Dickinson's poetry. She uses the word here and in two other poems (125 and 257) to set an experience she possesses in relation to one that is absent. The fading ratio of poem 88 is actually somewhat atypical in that it does not provide the normally confident estimate of the far term. The mathematics here is broken, both imperfectly executed and victimized by the incommensurability between the finite and the infinite.

According to Dickinson's lexicon, "ratio" derives in part from the Latin *reor*, meaning to set in the mind and also to speak. Computing ratios thus means deliberately positing and articulating the absent or unknown quantity. This notion pervades Dickinson's work, even where the word "ratio" is absent; almost every poem in which she counts, measures, reckons, or estimates something implies the idea. Often the ratio is direct, as of joy to joy in the celebratory nature poems or in love lyrics like "There came a day at summer's full." A negative or inverse ratio, one that measures earthly misery as an index of heavenly bliss or that counts secular blessings at religion's expense, is more common, however. This is the calculation implied in the many poems that advocate cultivating the "White Sustenance—/Despair—" (no. 640), for pain and despair inversely prefigure the glory to come. The negative ratio also appears in poems that praise distance or absence as guarantees of desirability. "Delight is as the flight—/Or in the ratio of it" (no. 257).

Dickinson is generally confident about her ability to compute ratios and about the benefits they afford her. A typical example of a successfully calculated ratio would be "that Etherial Gain/One earns by measuring the Grave—/Then—measuring the Sun—" (no. 574). The ratio falters, however, when a near term can no longer be grasped: "We let go all of Time/Without—Arithmetic of Him—" (no. 1184). The requirement for success is thus imaginative possession of at least one term. Only then can one forcefully calculate the forces beyond one's reach.

Imaginative possession is the aim of Dickinson's other main mathematical trope, "sum," a word that appears in nineteen poems. The term is almost always a synonym for bounty or possession, and it often implies the act of taking possession. In contrast to casual experiences or objects, a counted sum is inalienably one's own, like the "Two" of love in "Sweet—You forgot—but I remembered" (no. 523). Such a "Sum [will] be never hindered," in spite of the lover's forgetfulness and in spite of the direr "Decay of You," both the waning of the beloved's affection and the beloved's death. The idea of a sum thus acquires its special force from the implication that it entails or constitutes true appropriation.

Unlike Whitman or Melville, who are fascinated by the indefinite, Dickinson usually prefers an accurate count to a wild surmise. "Infinite" can even be a term of reproach in her verse, especially when it contrasts with some countable quantity. In poem 696 the reason is clearly that Dickinson equates the precisely counted with the genuinely owned:

> Their Hight in Heaven comforts not—
> Their Glory—nought to me
> 'Twas best imperfect, as it was—
> I'm finite—I cant see
>
> The House of Supposition
> The Glimmering Frontier that
> skirts the Acres of Perhaps
> To me—shows insecure—
>
> The wealth I had—contented me—
> If 'twas a meaner size—
> Then I had counted it until
> It pleased my narrow Eyes—

Just as algebra in poem 269 defends against pain, so summation can defend against a feared indefiniteness or uncertainty. Indeed, the defenses merge when calculation eases the pain of deprivation by transforming its uncertain duration into a possessed sum. Arriving at that sum can give one the near term for an inverse ratio, thereby making it possible "to learn the Transport by the Pain—" (no. 167). Or, as the speaker hopes in poem 511, it can make the deprivation bearable simply by assigning it precise definition:

> If I could see you in a year
> I'd wind the months in balls—
> And put them each in separate Drawers—
> For fear the numbers fuse—
>
> If only Centuries, delayed

I'd count them on my Hand,
Subtracting, till my fingers dropped
Into Van Dieman's Land

. . .

But, now, uncertain of the length
Of this, that is between,
It goads me, like the Goblin Bee—
That will not state—it's sting.

The odd thing about this unremarkable poem is that, even if the calculation were possible, the speaker would have to labor in order to preserve the reassuring numbers. This necessity may seem to go against the confidence Dickinson normally expresses in her calculations. In "The Zeroes—taught us—Phosphorus [that is, light and heat]" (no. 689), the inverse ratio indicated in the first line depends on a regular, invariable, and computable "power/Of Opposite—to balance Odd—/If White—A Red—must be!" Such power seems to manifest a natural law, the command of which requires only the skill to discover and construe it.

In question is the source of whatever reliability Dickinson's calculations have. To readers aware of the mathematical mysticism found in earlier literature, Dickinson's mathematics, and especially her notion of ratio, may suggest a Pythagorean or neo-Platonic cosmic measure. According to such a conception, the universe manifests an exact numerical order, which the adept can discover and thereby know the truth. Dickinson, however, seems to practice a more opportunistic sort of calculation. This is the kind that, since the time of Galileo, physicists have regularly practiced: use the formula in which the data can be made to fit but do not worry much about why it works.

Dickinson's calculations conform more readily to a Galilean project of gaining practical power over nature than to a Pythagorean one of acceding to an autonomous and essentially sacred order. The world may not bring forth a spiritual truth whose natural language is the number, but certain features of it can indeed be brought under control by crafty, forceful calculations. The desired numbers in poem 511 would give the speaker a comforting command over fate. The numbers are not, however, an independent or objective aspect of her destiny; left to themselves they would fuse into an indefinite quantity, one that belies any pre-existing regularity.

At the extreme, in order to bring the world under control, Dickinson's computations aggressively rearrange the existing world and established ideas of it. The sages in poem 271 are not objectively incorrect in calling this world small; it is only that their estimate depends on a hypothetical measurement of the plummetless well. Dickinson, however, decides in this poem to cast out supposed infinities, preferring the finite numbers she more easily commands. Elsewhere (no. 643), she herself corroborates the sage's view by valuing a possible infinity over a graspable sum.

> I could suffice for Him, I knew—
> He—could suffice for Me—
> Yet hesitating fractions—Both
> Surveyed Infinity—

The aggressive, even violent force of calculation is evident in the rare poems in which Dickinson imagines herself subject to it. Such a fate is one form of the plight in " 'Twas like a Maelstrom, with a notch" (no. 414):

> As if a Goblin, with a Gauge—
> Kept measuring the Hours—
> Until you felt your Second
> Weigh, helpless in his Paws—

The goblin threatens to violate Dickinson by taking her measure. Presumably a similar and similarly effective violence can accompany Dickinson's own computations.

The difference between Galilean and Pythagorean mathematics is hardly clear-cut, and I am not sure that Dickinson always holds to the former. The distinction does not map onto a simple opposition between the subjectively imposed and the objectively subsisting, for the test of Galilean mathematics is that within a carefully delimited sphere it does effectively apply. (The velocity of a falling body is independent of its density, for example, but only in an absolute vacuum, an idealized or imaginary space.) The matter may become clearer if we reexamine the lines from poem 689. The inverse ratio of "The zeroes taught us phosphorus" is not strictly mathematical, for it lies somewhere between the quantitative domain of the thermometer and a qualitative, a semantic realm expressed in the relationship of white to red. Contra Dickinson, white and red are not invariably opposite; probably most of us would balance white with black. More obvious than the mathematical then, the semantic ratio shows that Dickinson has intervened on and, as the saying now goes, cooked the data. But this manipulation produces a ratio that is indeed effective and reliable in the zone to which she applies it.

Understood as an aggressive force for possessing and controlling experience, mathematics might be expected to resemble what is otherwise most triumphantly Dickinson's own, her poetic language. Language would thus be like mathematics in being a mental construct rather than a faithful representation of what is given in and by nature. Poem 511 suggests the similarity in a negative way, identifying the failure of the speaker's calculations with the goblin bee that does not speak itself. The etymological bond between ratio and speaking further reinforces the suspicion. Poem 1668 seems to confirm it:

If I could tell how glad I was
I should not be so glad—
But when I cannot make the Force
Nor mould it into Word

I know it is a sign
That new Dilemma be
From mathematics further off
Than from eternity

The dilemma here is the familiar choice between eternity, apparently the source or destination of gladness, and selfhood, here identified with force, mathematics, and language. Unlike the more common typological response to the dilemma, however (where gladness would be the near term of an eschatological ratio), here the emotion is a contingency distinct from both self and heaven. Even gladness is thus alien until it has been appropriated by the made force of counting and wording.

Counting and wording are not identical, however. Unlike earlier poets, Dickinson does not use the traditional semantic resources of "number," "measure," or "figure," whereby each term can refer to both mathematical and poetic patterns (as well as natural ones, whose harmony with mental constructs is thus indicated). Given Dickinson's penchant for linguistic compression, the omission of these established conceptual puns is striking. It suggests that she finds numbers and poems to be as much different as they are similar.

Dickinson writes a poetry that is singularly removed from identifiable scenes and concretely represented situations. Whereas even so austere a purist as Mallarmé will name the flower's attributes before negating the object into a transcendent *azur*, Dickinson often begins with unlocalized abstractions, whose elided syntactic markers allow them to represent persons, things, qualities, states of mind, and actions all at once. Mathematical imagery extends this rarefication to the utmost, for in its "pure or speculative form," so her dictionary states, mathematics is the "science of quantity . . . without relation to matter."

Strictly speaking, even the phrase "mathematical imagery" is an oxymoron, for the terms of pure mathematics are intelligible without being sensible. There are some fairly straight edges in nature, but no lines. Mathematical terms are thus more fully independent of the material world than other abstract concepts. The words Dickinson most often refuses to localize—presence, beauty, possibility, and so on—all carry concrete semantic associations. Mathematical terms are words also, to be sure, and they do not wholly escape tangible semantic contexts. Indeed, given Dickinson's association of counting with power, she was probably aware of Noah Webster's etymology for "reckon." The word's Saxon root signifies "not only to tell or count but . . . to rule or govern."[15] Nevertheless, mathematical terms represent in Dickinson a purer ideality, one that is without relation to matter, as I have already quoted Webster for saying. It is this supposed or intended purity that has led modern mathematics away from verbalizable signs to the rigorously stipulated and hence antiverbal glyphs of symbolic notation.

Webster is one possible source or confirmation for the primarily speculative conception of mathematics Dickinson holds. She enjoyed an unusually thorough schooling in elementary mathematics, but, except for having studied geometry through a translation of Euclid, her education seems to have stressed the applied skills that nineteenth-century America prized most highly.[16] Nevertheless, in her poems Dickinson clearly distinguishes mathematical ideas from more concrete ones. Three different poems casually, and as if the matter were obvious, distinguish "globe" [that is, geography] from "logarithm," "history" from "mathematics," and "lexicon" from "logarithm" (nos. 433, 553, and 728). The first term in each pair refers to symbolic systems that represent the material world and thus constitute the normal stuff of poetry, even so unlocalized a variety as Dickinson's. The second term refers to the pure idealities of mathematics.

Mathematical ideas are further distinct from other mental constructs in that they are products of subjectivity and yet also, unlike wishes, fantasies, or introspective reflections, the putatively ideal form of objectivity. This, after all, is the traditional claim for mathematics as the queen of the sciences. Her allegedly unique bridge between inner and outer has trembled a bit in modern times, especially since the introduction of non-Euclidean geometries, but Nobel Prize winners continue to marvel at the inexplicable match between the physical universe and the systems of theoretical mathematics.

The special virtue of mathematics as a counterpower is thus that it does not abandon the outer world. It can thereby provide a sort of immunity to the solipsism that persistently threatens romantic idealism. As a result, Dickinson can convincingly and effectively pose mathematical ideas against the material claims of nature or society. More importantly (because Dickinson more regularly uses mathematical notions in this way), they can be posed against divine or daemonic power, whose one consistent attribute is indefiniteness or its quantitative equivalent, infinitude.

The specific role of mathematics in a poetics of power and of the sublime can best be seen in a series of poems that make use of two figures: the bird, traditional emblem of the naturally poetic, and "circumference," Dickinson's best known mathematical term. "Circumference" is a notoriously elusive word, one that includes some meanings I shall neglect, but it is frequently Dickinson's term for the mathematical idea as such and hence for the ideal realm mathematics proposes and inhabits. Metaphorically, it is also the poetic idea, as in her declaration that "My Business is Circumference" (*Letters* II, 268). The contrast between the claims of circumference and those of the orthodox sublime is implicit in another letter, which has sometimes tamely been taken as praise for scripture. "The Bible dealt with the Centre, not with the Circumference—" (*Letters*, III, 950). The Bible represents divine power and the canonical instances of sublime identification with it. Although always attracted by that center, Dickinson typically opts for circumference, which, in poem 798, designates a transcendence that is within the self's powers:

She staked her Feathers—Gained an Arc—
Debated—Rose again—
This time—beyond the estimate
Of Envy, or of Men—

And now, among Circumference—
Her steady Boat be seen—
At home—among the Billows—As
The Bough where she was born—

This may be the most impressively optimistic poem Dickinson ever wrote. The bird is able to trade the partial bliss of the arc for the soaring paradise of circumference, and she does this without needing to submit to some alien power or even to traffic much with anything outside herself. That the achievement is beyond our estimate seems likely, especially given Dickinson's ambivalence about counting the infinite, but the truly idealistic claim is that the feat is beyond envy. The bird's triumph is precisely what Dickinson everywhere testifies to desiring for herself and nowhere claims to have achieved so definitively.

Dickinson apparently identifies with the bird of 798; certainly it is difficult not to associate the bird's glory with her own or the poem's. A somewhat similar situation is depicted in "The Birds begun at Four o'clock" (no. 783), but there the triumphant birds seem more alien. As "independant Extasy/Of Deity and Men," the birds' chorus represents a majestic and wholly self-sufficient natural presence that for other romantic poets—notably Keats, Shelley, and Whitman—might have precipitated sublime identification. Dickinson is present in the poem as first-person speaker, and her response begins with the confusion and the sense of being overwhelmed that normally inaugurate the sublime. She even names the experience a flood. Her involvement largely ends with the inaugural moment, however, and with a recognition of the birds' independence: "I could not count their Force—." In one respect the line only indicates the birdsong's intensity. According to what we have noticed elsewhere, however, the line expressly acknowledges that the singing is beyond her power to appropriate. The poem refuses the sublime, in other words, admitting that its glory is beyond her.

Poem 783 is not likely to satisfy those for whom the sublime is the highest order of art, and it may not have satisfied Dickinson either. A poem dated 1866 by Johnson (three years after poem 783) seems to be a direct revision of it:

> At Half past Three, a single Bird
> Unto a silent Sky
> Propounded but a single term
> Of cautious melody.
>
> At Half past Four, Experiment
> Had subjugated test
> And lo, Her silver Principle
> Supplanted all the rest.
>
> At Half past Seven, element
> Nor Implement be seen—
> And Place was where the Presence was
> Circumference between.

Several changes from the longer poem are noteworthy. First, the uncounted flock that bursts into full song has been replaced by a single bird, who, like the one in 798, begins cautiously. Second, the bird's actions are described in the language of human intellectual endeavor and psychic combat rather than that of natural force; the bird propounds a term until it becomes a principle that subjugates and supplants. Third, the leisurely narrative of a morning's event has been replaced by a maniacally precise but oddly uninformative timekeeping. The sun—Dickinson's normal image for nature's dominion—has disappeared, replaced in effect by the abstract chronology, which no longer even distinguishes morning from evening. The chronology itself is thus an instance of Dickinsonian computation, in that it takes over from the natural interval. Furthermore, the rather copiously detailed scene of the earlier poem has been so emptied out that bird, sky, and poetic voice can truly be said to have supplanted all the rest. We have nearly arrived at Wallace Stevens's American sublime, "the empty spirit in vacant space."

There is still the bird, however. Dickinson's first response to it is to observe, as poem 783 had done, that the song accomplishes nothing. Where presence, the transfiguring power of the song's silver principle, had for a brief time flourished is now mere place, nature in all its mute and empty thereness. In contrast to the bird of 798, which never lands, this one and its predecessors are obliged to stop singing, leaving the silent sky much as it had been.

So far, except for the greater austerity of scene and voice, the poet's relation to the bird only echoes and perhaps mildly amplifies the begrudgement of 798. Dickinson's bolder response is to assert that circumference remains between. Her poetic or mathematic idea, in other words, although less potent than the birdsong, surpasses the normal force of nature. It also seems to triumph over the birdsong's impermanence, perhaps even abandoning natural temporality altogether. If one respects the mathematic force of the line ending, then—alone among the poem's events—circumference gets no time signature. Even if one reads less ingeniously and assumes that the poet has merely elided a "was" or that "Half past Seven" controls the entire stanza, circumference still remains in at least two senses: first, that the numerical chronology is already a function of circumference's dominion and, second, that circumference is by stipulation the realm of the poem itself. Where place and even presence had been, poem is.

Circumference thus designates the quasi-spatial destination of Dickinson's poetic achievement and the mathematical instrument that is one of her means for reaching it. The range of ambition implied by the term varies somewhat from poem to poem, but "At Half past Three, a single Bird" indicates the normal locus of the mathematical concept and hence of the triumphant poetic self. Dickinson stands most often precisely in a between of her own device, bracketed on the side she usually faces by power, some mighty agency demanding her subjection, and on the other by fate, the dreary place of unredeemed materiality. Occasionally the between is a mediation, partaking a bit of presence and a bit of place and therefore manifesting the benevolent triangulation Emerson imagines in cheerful moments. Elsewhere it is less a congruence of Freedom, Fate, and Power than a cry of triumphant freedom, a presentation or positing of the self's having overcome the seductive threat of power, escaped from fate, and founded a realm of its own. Finally, in light of Dickinson's never-concluded negotiations over the dowry to paid the bridegroom power, the between can be quasi-temporal, a precarious moment in which she lingers while considering her answer to the suit.

3. A Calculated Sublime

Two questions remain unanswered. That they are the ones with which I began is meant to express my caution about hastily enclosing Dickinson's work in a conceptual net. Every student of Dickinson's writings must be wary of a spurious reader's sublime. Her 1775 poems and 1171 collected letters and prose fragments are so numerous, so persistently enigmatic, and so free from ready-made hierarchies of importance or import that the reader in search of definitive answers may be condemned to that fate. One begins in amazed confusion, then grasps onto the seemingly legible, like Wordsworth singling out the blind beggar at Bartholomew Fair. But the vaunting sense of power that such focus may bring should not conceal a truth Harold Bloom has dwelt on: that the sublime is unthinkable without repression.[18]

The two pending questions are mutually exclusive. I have proposed that Dickinson practices a singular poetic strategy, that of the calculated sublime. Assuming for a moment the sublimity, is the strategy so distinctive? Has it not been anticipated, comprehended, and even put in its place by Kant, in the account of what he was first to call the mathematical sublime? If so, Dickingson's pursuit of a power that remains free of the sublime's normally submissive identifications must be seen as a deluded, even self-deceiving enterprise. On the other hand, mindful of the poet's hesitations at the edge of transcendence and of the bounds that circumference inscribes on poetic ambition, one must ask if she can truly be said to practice a sublime poetics, much less a poetics of power. The phrase "calculated sublime" is a contradiction in terms, after all, especially in light of the involuntary self-abandonment and the submissive identification I have stressed.

There are some similarities between Kant's analysis of the sublime and Dickinson's practice. Although he distinguishes the mathematical from the dynamical sublime, the rhetoric of power that is proper to the latter generally also gets employed for the former. Similarly, Dickinson almost always sees magnitude as an index of might. In addition, Kant's division of role between the imagination's esthetic apprehensions and reason's ideas resembles in important ways Dickinson's distinction between lexicon and logarithm. The first term in each pair refers to the representation of sensible images (and the concrete understanding of them); the second refers to the presentation of transnatural idealities.

The crucial question is the relation of Kantian reason to the faculty that produces circumference. Both appear to be transcendental faculties capable of triumphing over all natural limitations. But in Kant's sublime, the advent of reason means the discovery of a universal law. It thus seems incompatible with Dickinson's imperial insistence on freedom for all her faculties. In "Me from Myself—to Banish" (no. 642), one of several poems that stage a civil war among rival psychic agencies, it is clear that neither "mutual Monarch" will abdicate to the other.

Mathematics is hardly an exercise of lawless caprice, however, even when applied opportunistically. If it thus stands as a Kantian law to Dickinson, her freedom will have compromised itself in the very act of staking out a circumference of its own. Unwittingly or unacknowledgedly, Dickinson will have had to have identified with mathematics. Just as reason requires the subject Kantian faculties to identify with its hegemony, it thereby makes of the sublime a kind of interior coronation rite.

Dickinson writes a few poems (nos. 433 and 728) in which mathematics is portrayed as a fairly tiresome discipline one must undergo at school, but these tell us little. The only poem that seriously treats mathematics and selfhood is number 545:

> 'Tis One by One—the Father counts—
> And then a Tract between
> Set Cypherless—to teach the Eye
> The Value of it's Ten
>
> Until the peevish Student
> Acquire the Quick of Skill
> Then the Numerals are dowered back—
> Adorning all the Rule
>
> 'Tis mostly slate and Pencil
> And Darkness on the School
> Distracts the Children's fingers
> Still the Eternal Rule
>
> Regards each Cypherer alike
> With leader of the Band
> And every separate Urchin's Sum
> Is fashioned for his hand.

The poem insists upon the difference between mathematical skill and the patriarch who teaches it, that is, between the rules of mathematics and of the father. The ominous thing about reason in Kant's analytic is that it functions rhetorically as a personification, an agency engaged in power struggles with rival agencies. That role is taken here by the teacher, whose oppressive moral authority is wonderfully captured in the pun on "tract" and in the pronoun that makes the numeral ten belong to that authority. Mathematics itself, however, is an impersonal, egalitarian rule and hence a realm into which rivalries need not enter. Learning mathematics is the discovery, not that one must obey it, but that its sums are fashioned for one's hand. No submission to the father and no curtailment of freedom is required.

The crucial step is when numerals are dowered back. The verb phrase is a legal term meaning the return to a man's widow of that part of his estate originally belonging to her. Acquiring the quick of skill thus implies the death of the father, about whom one has perhaps suffered oedipal anxieties, and the discovery that numerals, the dowry, have belonged to one all along. The "identification" here is with an eternal rule that the pedagogue had usurped. Learning mathematics thus entails not identifying with it but recognizing it as a native endowment.

(It should be noted that this poem is vulnerable to a skeptical reading. For example, the rule of mathematics looks suspiciously like the fantasy parent of an urchin's family romance, especially considering the confusion of genders and generations traced by father, husband, widow, and male urchin.)

Rather than Dickinson's freedom or the cogency of her poetics, the second unanswered question challenges my claims about the relevance of the sublime if its orthodox mechanisms are absent. The warrant for retaining the "sublime" must arise not from the singular mechanisms in Dickinson's poetry but from the relation of her poetic project to the goals for which the sublime is generally honored or endured.

There can be little doubt that a large body of Dickinson's work, especially the poems that trace intensely agonizing psychic experiences, ought to be classed in the romantic sublime. Such poetry takes tremendous and genuinely inspiring risks, always with a view toward uniting the human and the transcendent. Those poems are not, however, the ones to which Dickinson's calculations most often apply. "Infinite" is usually an honorific term in the obviously sublime poetry, whereas we have noticed hostility or ambivalence to what cannot be counted. Accordingly, one might argue that most of the mathematical poems knowingly refuse the heights of sublimity or power. Circumference would then be a compromise or consolation, the realm one inhabits instead of daring to confront the center.

I do not think this would be an accurate judgment of the mathematical poems. (The exceptions, like "The Birds begun at Four o'clock" have been noted.) Dickinson's calculaton of sums and ratios is not a way of reserving risk and settling for a lesser glory but precisely a strategy for magnifying her powers and her freedom to exercise them. She clearly suspects the ruse of sublimity, whereby power is purchased at the cost of sacrificing one's freedom and then of repressing the origins of the power in order to persuade oneself that submission is a higher freedom. As poem 1461 sarcastically puts it, such a course means saying to the " 'Heavenly Father' " that "We apologize to thee/For thine own duplicity—." Dickinson's calculated sublime thus refuses not power but the decoy by which power extends its alien realm. She draws or measures the line of circumference not to shun danger but to mark the apocalyptic realm in which one dares the union of unconditional power and unconditional freedom:

> I saw no Way—The Heavens were stitched—
> I felt the Columns close—
> The Earth reversed her Hemispheres—
> I touched the universe—

And back it slid—and I alone
A Speck upon a Ball—
Went out upon Circumference—
Beyond the Dip of Bell— (no. 378)

Notes

1. A few more than one hundred of the references are pointed enough to justify saying that the poem turns on mathematical usage. The range is from technical terms like "decimal" to words like "reckon" and "measure" that need not be quantitative. The estimates here and throughout the essay derive from S. P. Rosenbaum (ed.), *A Concordance to the Poems of Emily Dickinson*, (Ithaca, N.Y.: Cornell University Press, 1964).

2. Thomas H. Johnson (ed.), *Letters of Emily Dickinson*, 3 vols. (Cambridge, Mass.: Harvard University Press, 1958), II, 631, letter no. 583. Subsequent references to the *Letters* will be cited by volume and letter number. Similar plays on the phrase from the Lord's Prayer can be found in *Letters*, II, 292 and II, 330.

3. For a general history of the sublime see Samual H. Monk, *The Sublime* (New York: MLA, 1935) or J. L. Boulton's introduction to Edmund Burke, *An Enquiry into the Origin of our Ideas of the Sublime and Beautiful* (London: Routledge and Kegan Paul, 1958).

4. *Letters*, III, 1042. Dickinson quotes the phrase correctly in "A little East of Jordon."

5. Joanne Feit Diehl argues that all three sources and also the interior agency sometimes called "consciousness" are versions of a single figure, the stranger, who is esentially a projection of inner forces. See Diehl's "Dickinson and the American Self," *ESQ* 26 (1980), 1–19 and "Emerson, Dickinson, and the Abyss," *ELH* 44 (1977), 683–700. Because Dickinson will occasionally play one figure off against another, however, I see no reason not to distinguish them.

6. The centerpiece of modern work on the sublime is Thomas Weiskel's partly psychoanalytic *The Romantic Sublime*

(Baltimore: Johns Hopkins Press, 1976). My debts to the book are numerous. The other important Freudian reflections on the sublime come from Harold Bloom. See especially *A Map of Misreading* (New York: Oxford University Press, 1975) and *Poetry and Repression* (New Haven: Yale University Press, 1976).

7. *Longinus on the Sublime*, translated by W. Rhys Roberts (Cambridge, Eng.: Cambridge University Press, 1899), 55.

8. For a summary of Freud's views on identification and a list of the many texts in which he discusses the idea, see J. Laplanche and J.-B. Pontalis *The Language of Psychoanalysis* (New York: Norton, 1973), 205–8. Weiskel (99–106) suggests that the oedipal pattern is a secondary mechanism overlaid on oral fantasies.

9. Immanuel Kant, *The Critique of Judgement*, translated by James C. Meredith (New York: Oxford University Press, 1952), 90–204.

10. See Sandra H. Gilbert and Susan Gubar, *The Madwoman in the Attic* (New Haven: Yale University Press, 1979), 581–650, as well as the articles by Diehl previously cited and her " 'Come Slowly—Eden': An Exploration of Women Poets and Their Muse," *Signs* 3 (Spring 1978), 572–87.

11. *Poems of Emily Dickinson*, edited by Thomas H. Johnson, 3 vols. (Cambridge, Mass.: Harvard University Press, 1955). Reference to the *Poems* will be by first-line title or poem number. I have sometimes normalized Dickinson's punctuation and syntax in the references.

12. Harold Bloom isolates the same triad, somewhat differently defined, and supplies an exhaustive list of variant names in *Wallace Stevens: The Poems of Our Climate* (Ithaca, N.Y.: Cornell University Press, 1977), 3–10.

13. Compare poem 1265 in which the bird's resumption of daily life is a loss of dominion and a return to the transitive estate. Dickinson's transitive here means primarily in transit from birth to death, but the poem as a whole insists, as do many others, on the absence of goals or objects at the moment of dominion.

14. Robert Weisbuch, *Emily Dickinson's poetry* (Chicago: University of Chicago Press, 1975).

15. Here and throughout the essay dictionary citations are from the 1847 edition of *an American Dictionary of the English Language* (Springfield, Mass.: Merriam).

16. A fair guess at the text books Dickinson used at Amherst Academy can be made from the book lists for 1838 and 1847 cited in Frederick Tuckerman, *Amherst Academy: A New England School of the Past, 1814–1861* (Amherst, Mass.: privately printed, 1929), 99–100, 114. They would have been (Daniel)) Adams's *Arithmetic*, Day's *Algebra*, and (John) Playfair's Euclid. Her Mt. Holyoke texts can be surmised from Mary Lyon's recommendations of 1835, twelve years before Dickinson matriculated. Lyon's list is quoted in Richard Sewall's *Life of Emily Dickinson* (New York: Farrar, Straus, and Giroux, 1974), II, 362. Adams and Playfair are on the college list; so also are an algebra by Baily (probably John Baily but possibly Francis Bailey) and an abridgement of Euclid by (Robert) Stimson. All of these widely used textbooks went through many editions in the eighteenth and nineteenth centuries.

17. Richard P. Feynman, *the Character of Physical Law* (London: British Broadcasting Co., 1965).

18. See especially *Poetry and Repression.*

Chapter 6

Kant and Stevens: The Dynamics of the Sublime and the Dynamics of Poetry

MICHAEL T. BEEHLER

Poetry is a search for the inexplicable

—Wallace Stevens

"How does one stand"[1] with respect to the "American sublime"? Or, more importantly for our purposes here, how does Wallace Stevens stand with respect to this figure that names a brief poem in the 1935 *Ideas of Order*? The term "sublime" occurs relatively infrequently in Stevens' poetry, with only "The American Sublime" and the first section of "Esthetique du Mal" reflecting any extended and explicit meditation on it. And yet there is at work in Stevens' poetry a dynamics of the sublime that underlies that poetry's continual circulation of ideas of language and poetry, and of metaphors of metaphor. In Stevens, the "sublime"—American or otherwise—names a particular movement within poetic language: the metaphor of a journey or passage—a "search"—in metaphor toward that which lies beyond the boundary of its own metaphoricity. In a repetition of Crispin's earlier voyage, the later poetry and prose figure this movement as a "sail" that investigates the marginal zone distinguishing the known from the unknown and the rational from the irrational. It is upon and within this margin that Stevens' poetry of American sublime is written.

The sublime in Stevens can be read with the help of a brief detour through the underworld (Stevens has called Plato, Aristotle, Hegel, and Kant "divinities of the Styx"[2]): Kant's book of the sublime, his *Critique of Judgement.* In his "Analytic of the Sublime," Kant associates sublimity with representations of infinity and boundlessness.[3] Here the sublime is that which we call "*absolutely great*" and which is therefore "*beyond all comparison*" (*Critique*, 106). In magnitude, for example, the *absolutely great* has only absolute scale, since it is wholly other than anything to which it might be compared. The sublime, then, presents itself literally in no thing, for "nothing . . . which can be an object of the senses, is . . . to be called sublime" (*Critique*, 109). Rather, the sublime names something always other than any object that can be sensually perceived: indeed, the Kantian sublime is in part a figure of absolute otherness, for "the sublime is that, the mere ability to think which, shows a faculty of the mind surpassing every standard of Sense" (*Critique*, 110). Since the sublime as such is never present in any object, Kant concludes that it is an effect occurring within the mind itself: "All that we can say is that the object is fit for the presentation of a sublimity which can be found in the mind; for no sensible form can contain the sublime properly so-called" (*Critique*, 103).

This last observation by Kant directs the argument toward the causes of the sublime effect, causes that relate specifically to a crisis of representation, for the Kantian sublime is that which cannot be "properly so-called." As Bernard Bosanquet pointed out just before the turn of the century, the sublime "in general [Bosanquet is reading Hegel reading Kant] is the attempt to express the infinite without finding in the realm of phenomena any object which proves itself fitting for this representation."[4] Thus in attempting to "express the infinite," to represent in a form or name the sublime which cannot be contained in any form or name, the imagination journeys to the very boundaries of representation only to discover there not the sublime properly so-called, but the inadequacy of representation itself.[5] In this sense, Kant explains, the sublime does "violence to the Imagination" which "reaches its maximum, and, in striving to surpass it, sinks back into itself" (*Critique*, 103, 112).

But in tracing the limits of representation, and thereby marking the difference or gap that forever separates the sublime from the set of all representations, the imagination travels a *via negativa* by which the absence represented by all (inadequate) representations of the sublime itself signifies the sublime *other* beyond representation's margins. The sublime thus appears (negatively) in the gesture by which representation marks its inability to represent, and is consequently a "reflection upon . . . representation": "we always . . . bind up with the representation a kind of respect, as also a kind of contempt for what we simply call 'small' " (*Critique*, 108). The sublime, in other words, arises within a particular hermeneutics of representation, an "attitude of thought" or "state of mind" that, by remarking on the fallenness of representation, "introduces subliminity into the representations of nature" (*Critique*, 104, 110). Kant will later note that both beauty and sublimity are "aesthetical modes of representation" (*Critique*, 138–39).[6]

It is this particular understanding of representation as fallen and inadequate that underwrites Kant's negative sublime by gesturing, as Thomas Weiskel has pointed out, toward what lies beyond the horizon of representation: "The sublime dramatized the rhythm of transcendence in its extreme and purest form, for the sublime began where the conventional systems, readings of landscape or text, broke down, and it found in that very collapse the foundation for another order of meaning."[7] In Kant's own terms, the failure of representation generates the drive to pass beyond representation's horizon and impels the imagination toward the abyss of the transcendent: "The transcendent (towards which the Imagination is impelled in its apprehension of intuition) is for the Imagination like a abyss in which it fears to lose itself" (*Critique*, 120). We shall for the moment overlook Kant's last image only to underscore this dynamic aspect of the negative sublime, in which the absence in representation inaugurates the impulsive drive toward the transcendent, and "the sensible in the representation of nature is judged available for a possible supersensible use" (*Critique*, 133). Kant's reference to Jewish law's prohibition on image-making is a precise figure of the dynamics of the sublime. He observes that "perhaps there is no sublimer passage in the Jewish Law than the command, *Thou shalt not make to thyself any graven image, nor the likeness of anything which is in heaven or on earth or under the earth*" (*Critique*, 143). This law is a succinct statement of the hermeneutics of representaton implicit in the negative sublime, for the interdict assures the fallenness of all writing and image-making, which in turn impulsively drives the imagination toward a transcendent divinity that appears as the interdict's source. It is by this circular means, then—by a writing that reflects within itself a gap that is taken to be the margin between writing and a transcendent outside—that the figure of the transcendent first appears.

Representation's gesture toward its own emptiness, however, can be subverted into the mark of an actual object or referent, and thus can be diverted from the dynamics of the sublime. This, for Kant, is the danger of *fanaticism*, which is "*a delusion that we can will ourselves to see something beyond all bounds of sensibility*" (*Critique*, 144). The sign of the transcendent— the emptiness of the representation—is fanatically filled by a delusional metaphor, and thus the impulsion toward the transcendent is provisionally cut off by a fiction. This is the "subreption" by which the sublime—which can only appear as a horizonal difference between representation and the wholly other—is attributed to "an Object of nature" (*Critique*, 119). As Paul Ricoeur notes about the discourse of Freud, "it seems that such a horizon, by a kind of diabolic conversion, inevitably tends to be transformed into an object."[8] For Kant, this subreption is a kind of protective sublimation, by which the imagination, fearing to lose itself in the abyssmal margin that is the mark of the sublime, "sinks back into itself, by which, however, a kind of emotional satisfaction is produced" (*Critique*, 112). We recall, however, that it is the very possibility of representation to be delusion—the interdict prohibiting the image's accuracy, which makes all representation potential *mis*-representation—that lies at the heart of the dynamics of the negative sublime. Thus, in a somewhat problematic fashion, the subreption that Kant describes as dangerous is in fact a precondition of the sublime moment, and the transcendent toward which this moment of representational failure impels us relies in turn on the always possible, fanatical sublimation of the impulsive drive. Like the transcendent itself, the impulse to journey beyond representation's horizon—the impulse toward the transcendent—arises within that horizon, and is produced by the sublime interdict, the story of the image's fallenness and inadequacy.

—— ——

The figures critical to Kant's *via negativa* of representation—his dynamics of the sublime—also inform Stevens' meditations on similar issues. Those figures—the horizon, the search, and the transcendent—are implicit concerns of the poet's 1937 essay, "The Irrational Element in Poetry," where Stevens considers the story of poetry's fallenness and its impulsive *via negativa* toward its outside: toward that which lies beyond the horizon of poetic language as a transcendent that the essay names equally the "irrational" and the "unknown." For Kant, the gap in itself toward which representation gestures in the sublime moment is the absence that impels us toward a transcendent beyond representation's horizon. It is this sublime gap that for Kant marked the transcendent in whose absence presence itself could be divined and that, for Stevens, appears as a repeated poetic figure. In this essay, the horizon that discloses the "beyond" of the transcendent—and thus the fallenness of the poetic image—reveals instead its own metaphoricity. For Stevens, the horizon of metaphor is always contained within another metaphor. The end of metaphor in a limiting boundary or margin thus marks not a signifying absence, but rather the return of metaphor itself.

After some introductory remarks, the essay opens with an anecdote: the story of a snowy Thanksgiving in Hartford and of the poet, lying in bed, hearing "the steps of a cat running over the snow under [his] window almost inaudibly."[9] This sound is, for Stevens, a figure of all "pretexts for poetry," of all sources that lie behind the poetic text itself: sources which, the essay later explains, the poet "grows completely tired of" in an exhaustion that drives him toward a desired "subject" (*OP*, 221). The anecdote of the poetic "pretext" begins to define the irrational as a "transaction [we will return to this word later] between reality and the sensibility of the poet" that is the source "from which poetry springs" (*OP*, 217). This "transaction," it must be noted, assumes a determining margin between its two sides, and thus operates within the horizonal logic of limits and boundaries.

The irrational Stevens refers to in the essay also manifests itself within this logic. Like Kant's transcendent, Stevens' "irrational" appears to be the wholly other to which his essay can only negatively refer. It lies, for example, beyond the boundaries of the proper name. As Stevens writes late in the essay: "I use the word irrational more or less indifferently, as between its several senses" (*OP*, 229), any one of which thus impels us toward a totalizing "irrational" that has no proper sensual image. Stevens here evades a definition of the irrational by multiplying its various "senses," a strategy he uses again in "The Noble Rider and the Sound of Words," where he shows nobility "unfixed," because "if it is defined, it will be fixed and it must not be fixed. . . . To fix it is to put an end to it."[10] Like nobility, the irrational appears as that which lies beyond the fixing (and therefore inadequate) boundaries of representation. To show the irrational unfixed is to repeat the *via negativa* of writing.

The subreption that in Kant turns the transcendent to which representational absence gestures into a delusional metaphor first appears in Stevens' essay as a sublimation that reduces the otherness of the irrational to a representable object within the horizon of writing. Stevens here refers to Freud as "one of the great figures in the world" that has arisen since his earlier Harvard years, and notes that "while he is responsible for very little in poetry . . . he has given the irrational a legitimacy that it never had before," presumably by putting into place a discourse that accounts for the irrational as a determinable subject and not simply as an absent presence (*OP*, 218–19). This passive allusion to Freud and his book of the irrational turns hostile, however, five years later in "The Noble Rider and the Sound of Words," where Stevens equates Freud with Descartes as two of a "great many people" who have "cut poetry's throat" (*NA*, 14). Since the irrational is, like Kant's sublime, that which cannot be properly so-called, its determination in a discourse is clearly a delusion similar to fanaticism. On the other hand, Stevens' fluctuating and unfixed definition of the irrational maintains the figure of the inexplicable at the center of his essay and thus reinscribes the margin between the rational and the irrational, the gap that his discourse must write in itself in order to gesture toward the irrational otherness beyond itself. In its emphasized reinscription of this gap Stevens' essay recalls the Emersonian sublime of "Nature" which, as Donald Pease has pointed out, "arises with the breakdown of a continuous 'determinate' relation between self and other until only *the gap between* remains."[11]

And yet it is the status of this originating margin that the essay finally calls into question. As the title of the essay reminds us, the irrational is an otherness that is never really *other*, since it is an irrational element *in* poetry, the name of a "particular process *in* the rational mind which we recognize as irrational in the sense that it takes place unaccountably" (my italics; *OP*, 218). The "irrational" that the essay has continually placed beyond the margins of definition and writing also, it now appears, takes its place within those very margins. The process is unaccountable, then, not because it is a transcendent *other* to which the essay can only mutely gesture in a *via negativa* of self-deprecation. Rather, by refusing to take place simply inside poetry or simply outside of it, the irrational appears as a process that erases the boundary between inside and outside by allowing it to be written only as a metaphor of a boundary. For Kant, the sublime moment of representational absence reified the horizon between the image and its *other*, and thus impelled the imagination toward a thinking of transcendence. But for Stevens, the very logic of the horizon—the structural foundation of the sublime and the transcendent—is already a poetic figure, an "unwritten rhetoric that is always changing and to which the poet must always be turning" (*OP*, 226). The essay, therefore, first images the horizon as a "transaction," a term that for Stevens' legal mind carries overtones of a document in writing. Indeed, the irrational arises as a figure in the text of history, for "there is . . . a history of the irrational element in poetry, which is . . . merely a chapter of the history of the irrational in the arts generally" (*OP*, 218).

The sense of the horizon or boundary as a metaphor within the discourse of poetry—or, in Stevens' phrase, "as part of the dynamics of poetry" (*OP*, 227)—is crucial to the final section of "The Irrational Element in Poetry," where the meditation on the dynamics of the known ironically rewrites Kant's dynamics of the sublime. The section opens with an equation that allows for a substitution of terms: "The irrational bears the same relation to the rational that the unknown bears to the known" (*OP*, 227). What follows is an intricate description of the dynamics of the known which is equivalent to the dynamics of poetry: "I do not for a moment mean to indulge in mystical rhetoric, since for my part, I have no patience with that sort of thing. That the unknown as the source of knowledge, as the object of thought, is part of the dynamics of the known does not permit denial" (*OP*, 228). The dynamics of the known involves two terms—the known and the unknown—and therefore a differentiating boundary between them. It is this boundary that allows the unknown to appear as that which lies over the horizon of the known, as its source and object. But it is precisely the *as* of metaphor that produces this boundary, since the unknown—the outside par excellence of the known—is a figure intended to be taken "*as* the source of knowledge, *as* the object of thought" (my italics). The unknown stands as an undeniable metaphor of otherness ("We accept the unknown even when we are most skeptical," writes Stevens—*OP*, 228) within the dynamics of the known, and thus points to the metaphoricity of the known's horizon, the figure of the boundary, or gap that allows the metaphor of otherness to subreptively gesture toward a transcendent other. The metaphor of the unknown as source and object thus becomes a sign of literal transcendence only through the mediation of another metaphor—that of the horizon, boundary, or gap—in the same way that, in one of Stevens' adagia, "god" becomes "reality": "There is no such thing as a metaphor of a metaphor. One does not progress through metaphors. Thus reality is the indispensable element of each metaphor. When I say that man is a god it is very easy to see that if I say god is something else, god has become reality" (*OP*, 179). Reality is an "indispensable element of . . . metaphor," but it is itself a figure produced by the passage of one metaphor into another, and is thus both a reinscription and an erasure of the horizon between metaphor and "reality." What for Kant was the sublime horizon of representation is for Stevens an undeniable and seductive movement within the horizonless dynamics of poetic metaphor.

The essay concludes with a discussion of those who would take literally poetry's metaphor of its horizon and thereby render divinely transcendent the purely figurative other named by the irrational. These Stevens calls "charlatans of the irrational": "there are those who, having never yet been convinced that the rational has quite made us divine, are willing to assume the efficacy of the irrational in that respect" (*OP*, 228). This sublimation is a divination, but it is also a reinterpretation of the fanaticism of Kantian sublimation—the substitution of a sensual object for that which transcends the boundaries of the senses—that Stevens had repeated in his earlier allusion to Freud. Stevens goes on to observe that "the rational mind, dealing with the known, expects to find it glistening in a familiar ether. What it really finds is the unknown always behind and beyond the known, giving it the appearance, at best, of chiaroscuro" (*OP*, 228). But the placing of the "unknown always *behind* and *beyond* the known" (my italics) reinscribes the known's horizon and thereby rewrites the metaphor in which the search for an unknown can take place. Thus the Kantian sublimation is really the reverse of a more original subreption that turns a figure within the dynamics of poetry into a gesture marking a beyond of poetry. This subreption is precisely what "Notes toward a Supreme Fiction" calls the "project for the sun," in which the sun "must bear no name" in order to be seen as a "name for something that never could be named" (*CP*, 381). For Stevens, then, the Kantian sublime—representation's *via negativa* that, by marking in the image its limiting horizon, impels us toward the transcendent and renders absence a sign of presence—is the subreption that is the beginning of poetic "invention" (*CP*, 380), the supreme fiction that allows poetry to be written as though it were a journey beyond itself, "a search for the inexplicable" (*OP*, 173). The horizonal boundary produces the known and the unknown, the rational and the irrational, metaphor and reality, representation and the transcendent, by discriminating between each two, but in Stevens this discrimination—the sublime and sublimating gap within representation—is the originating fiction of poetry.

—— ——

Stevens' meditation on the "dynamics of poetry," then, is an ironic rewriting of Kant's dynamics of the sublime, for while it repeats the *via negativa* of the sublime moment, it does so only to disclose the supposed metaphoricity of its central figure: the horizonal gap in representation, the blank spot or absence that, through a subreption of its status as metaphor, can be interpreted as the sign of transcendent presence. The return of the horizon to the inside of poetic metaphor—the deconstruction of its privileged status as a literal boundary beyond which metaphor cannot pass—has two apparent consequences. First, since the limiting horizon of poetry is itself never other than a metaphor within poetic discourse, the outside of that discourse—which can be defined only as that which lies beyond the horizon—discloses itself as, originally, a poetic metaphor. Poetry's gesture toward what lies beyond itself is thus possible only in the context of another poetic figure, the one that stages the fiction of the horizon and, in turn, allows the "inside" and the "outside" to be thought.[12] The second consequence concerns Stevens' epigrammatic observation that "poetry is a search for the inexplicable" (*OP*, 173). Since the "inexplicable" is the name for that which exceeds the boundaries of discourse, this statement can be read as a reification of the romantic quest or journey, an impulsion to discover what lies beyond the horizon of poetry. But since this horizon is itself a metaphor, the search or journey beyond the boundaries of the explicable—beyond the borders of language itself—is never other than a circulation within language's illimitable space.[13] Thus in Stevens the sublime, the Kantian moment of the impulsion toward the transcendent, marks not the fallen limitation of representation and metaphor, but rather their boundless pervasiveness.

Stevens' poetry is nevertheless filled with explorers who go in "search of the inexplicable" and whose journeys disclose the metaphoric margin that allows their figurative passage to take place. Crispin is Stevens' early figure of such a voyager, but his most extended meditation on the journey—and the sublime impulsion "outward" toward transcendence—takes place through the figure of Ulysses, the "interminable adventurer" (*CP*, 520). The archetype of all voyagers, Ulysses appears in two of Stevens' late poems, "The World as Meditation" and "The Sail of Ulysses" (which, in an edited form, becomes "Presence of an External Master of Knowledge"). Both poems repeat the dynamics of the sublime—the horizon and the impulsion toward that horizon's transcendence—as a figure staged by the horizonless dynamics of poetry.

"The World as Meditation" focuses on the moment of Ulysses' return to Penelope in order to disclose that moment as a constantly repeated return to the metaphorics of the name. The poem only figuratively moves toward a resolution of the question that opens it, "Is it Ulysses that approaches from the east?"—a question marked by the "horizon" formed by Penelope's veiling "cretonnes" (*CP*, 520). It is this horizon that locates the apparent boundary between the artifice of composition—Penelope "has composed, so long a self with which to welcome his"—and its outside figured here as Ulysses' "savage presence":

Someone is moving

On the horizon and lifting himself up above it.
A form of fire approaches the cretonnes of
 Penelope,
Whose mere savage presence awakens the world in
 which she dwells.

This image of the form appearing on the horizon recalls an earlier poem, "A Primitive Like An Orb" (*CP*, 440–43), in which the form is a "giant of nothingness" always evolved by a discourse of desire as the sign of what lies beyond its boundaries: "the obscurest as, the distant was" that is "always too heavy for the sense/To seize." But this "giant," and the horizon that it marks, is simply the "fated eccentricity" of "the lover, the believer and the poet," whose "words are chosen out of their desire":

> Here, then, is an abstraction given head,
> A giant on the horizon, given arms,
> A massive body and long legs, stretched out,
> A definition with an illustration, not
> Too exactly labeled, a large among the smalls
> Of it, a close, parental magnitude,
> At the centre on the horizon, concentrum, grave
> And prodigious person, patron of origins.

We hear in this passage the Kantian sublime that binds up "with the representation a kind of respect, as also a kind of contempt for what we simply call 'small' " (*Critique*, 108), but the Stevensian "giant"—the echo of the Kantian absolutely great—results from a circulation of poetic texts in which "one poem proves another" as a "definition" supported by an "illustration." The "giant on the horizon" seems to mark the limiting border of poetry but is never other than a metaphor of that impossible horizon and therefore a sign not of poetry's transcendent outside, but of its illimitable inside. An "illusion" of a transcendent and totalizing whole, he discloses himself as a part of "the total/Of letters, prophecies, perception, clods/Of color"—part, that is, of the dynamics of poetry.

This giant, the sign of a horizon that is always being erased, like the "essential poem at the centre of things," both "is and . . ./Is not and, therefore, is," and thereby looks forward to Ulysses whose form "was Ulysses and it was not." In "The World as Meditation," Ulysses is another manifestation of the giant, but he too appears as an irreducible duplicity that discloses the fiction of "mere savage presence" by again marking the artifice of the horizonal "cretonnes." The meeting between "friend and dear friend," the return of Ulysses, is staged only by the repetition of the name that, by "never forgetting him that kept coming constantly so near," reinscribes in itself the figurative absence that can then appear as the sign of "mere savage presence."

The later poem of the "interminable adventurer," "The Sail of Ulysses" (*OP*, 99–105), is staged as a dramatic monologue by its opening and closing italicized sections. As a meditation on knowledge, the known, and the unknown, the poem echoes Stevens' earlier essay on the irrational, and extends the figure of the search that had found expression in, among other works, Tennyson's "Ulysses," who desires "to follow knowledge like a sinking star,/Beyond the utmost bound of human thought."[14] The Ulysses Stevens' poem discloses is such a "seeker," an explorer not only in the boundaries of human thought, but also in the fictive horizons of legend and metaphor.

A discussion of the mediations written in the poem's frame of italics must be deferred until a later moment in our argument. Within that frame, however, we find in the first four sections of the poem a meditation on the status of knowledge, one which reflects the impulsive desire of Ulysses to pass, as Tennyson had written, through the boundaries of the known. The sail of Ulysses thus traces a passage or bridge that, by transcending the horizon of the known, seeks to discover the presently unknown. Within the known's horizon, the unknown is apparently marked only by absence, and it is this absence that—in a reflection of Kant's negative sublime—impels Ulysses outward. In the poem's second canto, this impulsion is toward a desired closure of the circuit of speech:

> There is a human loneliness,
> A part of space and solitude,
> In which knowledge cannot be denied,
> In which nothing of knowledge fails,
> The luminous companion, the hand,

> The fortifying arm, the profound
> Response, the completely answering voice.

The images here are those of companionship, substantial support, and vocal response: figures of a joining in a totalized circuit of speech that overcomes the "human loneliness" of "space and solitude." These figures are, however, only "felt" as absences within that loneliness, since they are the "aid of greatness *to be* and the force" (my italics). As in the dynamics of Kant's *via negativa* of representation, these felt figures of a complimentary outside to "human loneliness" generate Ulysses' search by providing the "inner direction on which we depend."

The "true creator, the waver/Waving purpling wands" is the third canto's trope of this deferred greatness, one which will arise when the circuit of speech is closed, the horizon of "human loneliness" transcended. The image is of the dominant, creative, romantic self (a figure repeated by the "unnamed creator" of the fourth canto and the master of the sixth): the "quiet lamp" that, "creating from nothingness," reflects the "joy of meaning in design/Wrenched out of chaos." We hear in this figure the "blessed rage for order" of "The Idea of Order at Key West," the

> maker's rage to order words of the sea,
> Words of the fragrant portals, dimly-starred,
> And of ourselves and of our origins,
> In ghostlier demarcations,
> Keener sounds (*CP*, 130).

This early poem reflects the same desire for "the completely answering voice" that is the impulsive "force" behind Ulysses' voyage. In the appearance of the "true creator" the desire would find satisfaction, the joining of the voice with an answering "luminous companion" from beyond its horizon.

The journey outward, then, is a voyage toward the sun, that luminous companion that stands as a figure of central transcendence and otherness. It is a journey, as the fourth canto implies, beyond the boundaries of the "mystical": a demystifying, epistemological voyage toward a literal truth that, when known, will bring

> A freedom at last from the mystical,
> The beginning of a final order,
> The order of man's right to be
> As he is, the discipline of his scope
> Observed as an absolute, himself.

This journey toward the literally true thus appears as a voyage out from the eccentricities of fiction toward the "center of the self," man "as he is." And yet the terminus of the voyage in a pure, demystified "beginning" is, as the extended mediation that opens the canto indicates, never other than a beginning again within the horizon of metaphor:

> The unnamed creator of an unknown sphere,
> Unknown as yet, unknowable,
> Uncertain certainty, Apollo
> Imagined among the indigenes
> And Eden conceived on Morningside.

The desired center of knowledge marks not a freedom from the "mystical," but rather a return of the "imagined" and "conceived," just as, in "Notes toward a Supreme Fiction," the unmediated perception of the sun in its "remotest cleanliness" reveals only the conception of that sun as the invented "idea of it" (*CP*, 380). Desiring the "center" beyond the horizon of the "mystical," Ulysses searches for what is originally a mystifying metaphor. The hypothesis that opens his soliloquy conceals this subreption disclosed in the fourth canto, for its belief in the unity of being, and knowing is based on the structure of figurative language itself. Its horizon is the logic of metaphoric substitution (being for knowledge) and metonymic expansion ("to know one man is to know all"). It is only within this horizon that knowledge—the "only sun of the only day"—takes place. The search for what lies beyond the horizon of the "mystical" is thus a figure within the illimitable margins of a poetic language whose boundaries are themselves never other than delusional metaphors.

The forever foretold closure of Ulysses' passage through metaphor appears in canto five specifically as a closure of symbolic language on the thing symbolized, the object lying over the horizon of the symbolic. This is the life that is "always . . . another life,"

> A life beyond this present knowing,
> A life lighter than this present splendor,
> Brighter, perfected and distant away,
> Not to be reached but to be known,
> Not an attainment of the will
> But something illogically received,
> a diviniation.

Knowledge of this "perfected" life comes as a "divination," as a magical revelation of the life that transcends the boundaries of the present but imperfect "splendor." The "life" is that of demystified, totalizing truth, the "omnium" that descends

> the day on which the last star
> Has been counted, the genealogy
> Of gods and men destroyed.
> The ancient symbols will be nothing then.
> We shall have gone behind the symbols
> To that which they symbolized.

The canto ends, however, with a startling qualification, for on that day we shall have journeyed "Away/From the rumors of the speechfull domes" to another "chatter that is then the true legend." The passage is not beyond the horizon of symbol, but only within a symbology that retells legends of its horizon only to disclose the metaphoricity of any such limiting margin. The "divination" is the story of symbolic language's literal outside, but that outside—and therefore the felt imperfection of the symbol that, in a repetition of the Kantian moment of representational absence, impels Ulysses to search for it—is already part of the legend. The figure of the legend in this canto is like a similar legend in "The Green Plant" (*CP*, 506). There, it is only by looking "at the legend of the maroon and olive forest" that the "outside of the legend" glares "with the barbarous green/Of the harsh reality of which it is part." Here the "harsh reality," like the outside of the symbol, is simply another figure within the legend by which it symbolizes its fictive outside. The story of the symbol's fallen inadequacy—repeated by the Kantian sublime—is thus a critical fiction told by the legend about itself, the subreption by which the metaphor of its limiting horizon is brought into play.

The genealogy of symbols, whose end was foretold in canto five, returns in the sixth canto as the only possible space of knowledge:

> The mind renews the world in a verse,
> A passage of music, a paragraph
> By a right philosopher: renews
> And possesses by sincere insight
> In the John-begat-Jacob of what we know,
> the flights through space, changing habitudes.

It is this genealogical pattern, the repeated metaphysics of origins, fathers, and generations, that becomes the "law" for which canto seven provides several "manifestations." Each manifestation repeats, "always and always," a structure in which "particulars" are bent "to the abstract," and are made to organize themselves around that abstraction as though it were their center and origin:

>   the difficult inch,
> On which the vast arches of space

Repose, always, the credible thought
From which the incredible systems spring,
The little confine soon unconfined
In stellar largenesses.

Each figure is a return of the "giant," a return of the image of a transcendent presence lying beyond—or beneath, as a controlling center—the "incredible systems" it fathers.[15] But each simply repeats the law of genealogy whose end canto five has foretold. Although there is no "poet's ease of mind" in this "relative sublime"—in which the search for the outside of the symbol is a legendary passage that only circulates among symbols—its appearance is nevertheless the effect of the "fate that dwells in truth," the "coaxings" of a language itself the impels the search. For, as an earlier poem asked, "Where was it one first heard of the truth?" Its answer, "The the," marks the erasure of "truth" in its return to the "dump" of images. "Is it a philosopher's honeymoon, one finds/On the dump?" (*CP*, 203). Hardly—but the dump cannot be left behind, since its horizons are already part of its imaged trash.

The final canto of the poem reflects another manifestation of the coaxing "law" of canto seven. The old figure of the "giant"—the metaphor of transcendent presence and sibylline author of all divinations and texts—had been the "englistered woman," but Ulysses is satisfied that he has now left that worn out "old shape" behind:

What is the shape of the sibyl? Not,
For a change, the englistered woman, seated
In colorings harmonious, dewed and ashed
By them: gorgeous symbol seated
On the seat of halidom.

The new shape which plays the role of sibyl—and comes as Ulysses' discovery of the literally true beyond the horizon of symbol and metaphor—is "the sibyl of the self,/The self as sibyl." This substitution, however, does not result in the arrival of the self "as he is," as had been foretold by canto four. Rather, it is the return of the self *as* sibyl, the self as newest symbol of a sibylline authority that is kept in play only by the repeated circulation of symbols. In the final lines of the canto, the subreption of the worn out symbol, the "englistered woman," follows the "project for the sun" of "Notes toward a Supreme Fiction" (*CP*, 381) by becoming the sign of a "still inhuman more," of a transcendent *other* projected by "our features, known/And unknown." This is the final sublimation of the poem, a divination—in the sense of "making divine"—of the human in a symbol that is then "seen" as a sign of transcendence. Through this subreption the "unknown" and "inhuman more," and therefore the figure of the horizon of the human and the symbolic, is written again into the soliloquy of Ulysses, an inscription that repeats—as poetry's strategy—the dynamics of the sublime, and the impulsion toward the transcendent that continues the metaphoric "search," the project of poetry.

Ulysses' search for the unknown—for the "luminous companion" to the symbolic—is thus not a passage beyond the horizon of symbol, but is rather a continual rewriting of that horizon as a return to symbol, a return that is therefore the erasure of symbol's "outside" and the "horizon" that marks it. Stevens' story of Ulysses is the legend of this search, and of the legendary and of legend itself: a story that can be told only in quotation marks by a speaker who is himself a legendary "symbol of the seeker." The story is framed by the enigma of its italics, the poetic "outside" of the poem of the search that, by its intertextual mediations—a "symbol" reading the text that is "his own mind"—marks the journey itself as the textual legend of poetry's search and discovery. The enigma "alive" in the soliloquy always appears, like the negative sublime in Kant, as the mark of a transcendent other: "As if another sail went on/Straight forwardly through another night." But this mark—the sublime absence in representation—is for Stevens already part of the "as if" of metaphor, for the horizon of metaphor is never other than a metaphor of horizon. The dynamics of the sublime rely on a logocentric interpretation of the absence in representation as a sign of transcendent, unrepresentable presence. But for Stevens, this "absence" is already a staging in the legend and is a part, therefore, of the dynamics of poetry.

Notes

1. *The Collected Poems of Wallace Stevens* (New York: Knopf, 1954, 130. References to this text, cited as *CP*, will be made parenthetically in the body of the essay.

2. *Letters of Wallace Stevens*, edited by Holly Stevens (New York: Knopf, 1966), 476.

3. *Kant's Critique of Judgement*, translated by J. H. Bernard (London: Macmillan, 1914), 102, 116. References to this text, referred to as *Critique*, will be made parenthetically in the essay.

4. *A History of Aesthetic* (London: George Allen and Unwin, 1892), 356.

5. "For there is here a feeling of the inadequacy of his Imagination for presenting the Ideas of a whole" (*Critique*, 112). Kant reiterates this idea four pages later (*Critique*, 116).

6. Thomas Weiskel has accurately defined the Kantian hermeneutics ot representation: "In the Kantian moment of the sublime the surface is broken, the discourse breaks down, and the faculties are checked or suspended." *The Romantic sublime: Studies in the Structure and Psychology of Transcendence* (Baltimore: Johns Hopkins, 1976), 21.

7. Ibid., 22.

8. *Freud and Philosophy: An Essay on Interpretation*, translated by Denis Savage (New Haven: Yale University Press, 1970), 529.

9. *Opus Posthumous*, edited by Samuel French Morse (New York: Knopf, 1957), 217. References to this text, cited as *OP*, will appear parenthetically in the essay.

10. *The Necessary Angel: Essays on Reality and the Imagina-*

tion (New York: Random House, 1951), 34. References to this text, cited as *NA*, will appear parenthetically in the essay.

11. "Emerson, *Nature*, and the sovereignty of Influence," in *boundry 2*, 8, 3, 58.

12. For a discussion of metaphoric staging, see Joseph N. Riddel, "Metaphoric Staging: Stevens' Beginning Again of the 'End of the Book,' " in *Wallace Stevens: A Celebration*, edited by Frank Doggett and Rober Buttel (Princteon, N.J.: Princeton University Press, 1980), 308–38.

13. For more on the fiction of the journey, see the chapter on Wallace Stevens, "Fiction, Risk, and Deconstruction: The Poetry of Wallace Stevens," in Paul A. Bové, *Destructive Poetics: Heidegger and Modern American Poetry* (New York: Columbia University Press, 1980), 181–216.

14. *Poems of Tennyson*, edited by Jerome H. Buckley (Boston: Houghton Mifflin, 1958), 67.

15. In this section, Stevens rewrites the image of the "pack on a giant's back" from "Recitation After Dinner" (where Aeneas "bears upon his back/The father that he loves"—*OP*, 87) and the "majestic mother's flocking brood," in which the "mother's face,/The purpose of the poem, fills the room," from "Esthetique du Mal" (*CP*, 413).

Chapter 7

White Mythology and the American Sublime: Stevens' Auroral Fantasy

MARY ARENSBERG

You remain the more than natural figure. You Become the soft-footed phantom, the irrational Distortion, however fragrant, however dear.

—*Wallace Stevens*

For Wallace Stevens, the poetic process is a fantasy of desire or lover's discourse that invents the poem. The poem is an appointed meeting or "intensest rendezvous" which never takes place between the inventor of the discourse, the poet, as collector of differences, and the "lover who lies within the self," his invented fiction for otherness. He calls her his "interior paramour."[1] Throughout the *Collected Poems*, we can trace what J. Hillis Miller calls "a shadowy psychodrama" taking place between these two figures who have inhabited Stevens' "central mind": the feminine interior paramour or doubled beloved and her mate, the major man, Stevens' fictionalized self.[2] They appear in the poetry from the beginning, first as friends, then as lovers to become, in the late poem, "Final Soliloquy of the Interior Paramour," "one thing . . . a light, a power, the miraculous influence."

Recent readers of Stevens, revising their theories of presence in the poetry, reject the notion that there is an ideal presence or presences outside the text either as imagination, reality, self, other, or imagination. Presence in Stevens' poetry is an illusion, a seeming constructed within a linguistic hall of mirrors as the poet plays with the contours of language. And since presence is fictionalized, appearing and then reappearing from an abyss of words, it is extremely difficult to grasp the veiled, evasive feminine fiction which behaves like the double or döppelganger in the fiction of Nabokov, Poe, or Conrad. Her shadowy self eludes our grasp; we feel and briefly know her, but our knowledge of her has been baseless. As Stevens writes in "Description Without Place": "In the golden vacancy she comes and seems to be on the saying of her name" (*CP*: 339).

In the early period of *Harmonium*, the psycho-sexual relationship between the poet and his paramour remains for Stevens the most accessible expression to represent his method of composition. However, the paramour functions in the poetry as much more than a therapeutic substitute for erotic desire or as a vehicle of sublimation. For this poet, she is the ancient voice of the oracle who helps her poet remember present and remembered beauty and brings both pleasure and pain. She is the inhabitant of the inner sanctum of the poet's mind, the sybil in her cave, sending messages of instruction. As an invented fiction, it is not coincidental that the figure corresponds with Stevens' stated criteria for the making of the supreme fiction: she is abstract, like being, a presence without a place. She must also change and does, at once Eve in "Le Monocle de Mon Oncle," an aging Venus in the "Emperor of Ice-cream," or the dreaming woman of "Sunday Morning." And she certainly brings pleasure, not only through her metaphoric changes, but in the pale fire of her absence which sheds its magic on the best of Stevens' early poems.

After *Harmonium* and *Blue Guitar* and into *Ideas of Order* and *Parts of A World*, Stevens' poems begin to contain their own commentary and disclose their own nonliteralness and ontological impossibility. Now the paramour discards the garments of her adolescence to become a fiction for figuration itself. During his major phase, as Harold Bloom had commented, "Stevens has given us a canon of poems more advanced as *interpretation* than our criticism has yet gotten to be."[3] In fact, the criticism running through these later texts not only mimics the endless turnings of Heiddeger's "hermeneutical circle," but looks back toward Freud and Nietzsche while gesturing toward Derrida and beyond. Thus the psychodrama of poet and paramour in the post *Harmonium* or more deconstructive phases of the canon dramatizes its three major quests: 1. the failed attempt to break through imaginative repetition and break through to a primary firstness or what Stevens calls "the first idea"; 2. the doomed search for transcendence and disclosure (to be in touch with essence or realize sublimity); and 3. the attempt to recover lost origins and enact the fantasy of the primal scene.

While all or most of the texts are engaged in these quests for a "supreme fiction," their enterprise is doomed from the start, as the paramour remains trapped within what Michael Beehler calls "the rhetoric of a logocentric metaphysics."[4] She lives, in these texts, perpetually on the edge of fulfillment, a Cinderella, waiting for "being to come true." For she represents what a trope can never do or be: that is to break through the matrix of metaphoricity and gaze on poetry's extralinguistic source. Yet to gaze on the extralinguistic for Stevens would be to look upon nothingness. "There was never a world for her" or for Wallace Stevens, for that matter, only the pleasure of merely circulating in a world of words without place.

In his reading of *Freud and Philosophy*, Paul Ricoeur, while discussing the "integration of death into life," reminds us that both literature and folklore disclose a series of the "choice of the third woman" episodes in which the hero opts for the third figure.[5] We may ask, who is this third woman, this form who loves in silence, and whose beauty surpasses the other two by far? For Paris, she was Aphrodite, death bringing Venus; for Cinderella's Prince, she is the dream with whom he will spend the rest of his days; she is Atropos, the dumb fate of the trio, blind in her love and always welcoming. This third woman is death, "the mother earth who receives him once more."[6] Walt Whitman understood this choice. In "Out of the Cradle Endlessly Rocking," the poet's acceptance of the life-death rhythm depends most on the voice of the "undertone," that low mumbling of "the savage old mother" who reclaims her child like Ishmael awash on a bark of unsatisfied love. This "delicious word" of the death of mother, however, in Freud, in Whitman, and as we shall see in Stevens, is not voiced by a fantastic or regressive figuration, but is uttered silently within the confines of a "parental space" (Stevens) that reaches beyond the pleasures of family romance into the nameless realm of the reality principle, or the acceptance of the life rhythm into death.

The first woman is of course the originating parent, the unseparated archetype and Stevens' "timeless mother" of *Harmonium.* She gave birth to the fiction of the beloved mate chosen from the mother pattern and seemed to be like the body of the world in spring. And although the poet-son is never able to satisfy his yearning love for the mother of origins, he keeps perpetuating that absence in his attempts at marriage with the fictive mate, the interior paramour. The beloved paramour, then, in all her shapes and guises, is an invention to repeat the original mother (nature), whose own nature has never been known. The mother's breast is always the absent matrix against which the poet "phantomizes presence"; just as Stevens' earthly mother fiction carries within her "aspic nipples" both the poison and the curative to perpetuate the illusion of presence.[7] Their venom is the knowledge of an ever-absent love (the signified word), while their honey is the stuff of which fictions of presence are made. Thus the pain and anxiety suffered with the loss of the mother give way to the pleasures of inventing another female presence who (n)ever takes her place. This second woman, who reaches her apotheosis in *Notes*, is the "green, fluent mundo," the female presence whose absence predicates poetry.

In the last canto of *Notes*, however, the haunting of the paramour begins: she is becoming already "the soft-footed phantom . . . however fragrant, however dear." The first inkling of the transformation from a muse to a death mother, from a trope of presence-trace to a figure of absence-memory, occurs in the final stanza of Canto Eight:

> These external regions, what do we fill them with
> except reflections, the escapades of death,
> Cinderella
> fulfilling herself under the roof?

The difficulty and strangeness of this passage derive from the poet's linking of the ultimate dream fantasy, the Cinderella story, with defensive reactions against death. What is the relationship between the poet's troping against death and the Cinderella Story? In a sense, if we look at the Cinderella narration more closely, it becomes not only a tale of rags to riches and transformations but essentially a myth of origins and their displacement. For it is the story of a young girl (paltry nude) whose natural mother is deceased and who lives in poverty. She bears the burden of her poverty with patience and with grace until, through supernatural intervention, she is transformed into a princess as her wishes are fulfilled. Her dream of someday meeting her prince is actualized when she puts on the fictive clothing of magic and dances within the mirror world of the prince's ball. The fiction is sustained until the postmidnight world when her fictive self disappears and only its trace is left in the shoe of glass. The final crossing of the tale occurs when the girl is rescued through the trace and is ultimately cast into a position that is equal to or superior to the status into which she was born.

Cinderalla's fate is mirrored and echoed in the course of the interior paramour, for the muse is invented and fictionalized precisely because her origins are unknown. She springs from a place where the mother has already been lost, from those "external regions" where "nothingness is a nakedness," "a poverty, a point," as Stevens says in *Notes*, "where fact could not progress as fact." The "hour of inexpressible bliss" does not proceed from the fact of the mother but from the fact that the mother is never known. And the only place the lovers meet is the mirrored hall of the text where "love's characters" (letters) come face to face. The Cinderella ball is sustained in *Notes Towards A Supreme Fiction* as long as the paramour keeps revolving in her crystal; yet in the post-midnight world after *Notes*, the crystal breaks and only its trace, the shoe of glass, a thing of nothingness, remains as residue.

This Cinderella trace, the invisible shoe of glass which fits but "is a thing of ether," becomes the idiom of Stevens' third woman, the death goddess or haunted muse of the *Auroras* section. She makes her first appearance in the title poem of the volume as the fictionalized presence of the mother who receives her son once more. In "The Theme of the Three Caskets," Freud distinguishes this third woman from her original when he writes: "But it is in vain that an old man yearns for the love of a woman as he had it first from his mother: the third of the Fates alone, the silent goddess of death, will take him into her arms."[8] The embrace of this third woman is not only the enclosure of man in the death clasp but the recloaking of the illusion of the self within the shawl of memory. Memory , like this third muse, becomes, for Stevens, the force of absence, a trace for that otherness, that self whose centrality was an illusion.

"It is an illusion we were ever alive in the house of mothers," Stevens wrote in a later poem, confirming his belief that the maternal presence and closure, for that matter, are fictions themselves, but nevertheless illusions of desire. The third woman, a casket, is a leaden vessel which, according to Freud, houses a portrait of the bride; like memory, this female crypt ("the owl in the sarcophagus") silently repeats the fictions of the past and distorts these "dark forms of desire" within the abysses of thought. The portrait of the fictive bride is memory's copy of an original presence that was absence anyway, enclosed within those nameless edges the poet calls oblivion. Stevens' haunted muse, the memory, is the mother of us all in the sense that rememberance gives birth to fictions of the self. Memory fabricates presence from the baseless forms of fictions that never were.

It is curious, then, that as the *Auroras* opens Stevens' reader is plunged into a foreign landscape which strikes us as both alien and familiar, like a dream. The basic dream of the opening of the poem is of phallic movement within a female environment:

> This is where the serpent lives, the bodiless,
> His head is air. Beneath his tip at night
> Eyes open and fix on us in every sky.

The "this" in the first line of the text presents us with its first problematic element, for, like its cousin, "the, the," in "The Man on the Dump," it is a demonstrative pronoun in obvious search for its subject. We can supply the subject quite readily as many of Stevens' readers have: Harold Bloom refers us to *Notes* and its line, "from this poem springs, that we live in a place that is not our own." Joseph Riddel identifies the enigma with textuality and metaphor itself, the aberrant sign or symbol for the limitation of language."[9] I would suggest that with the opening of the *Auroras*, Stevens has plunged us, belatedly to be sure, into the realm of the primal dreamer where sexual difference and *differance* are genitalized into a trope for death. The "this" in the opening line is a linguistic trace which fails to refer to the principle of the mother, at the same time it points toward the feminine nature of the text, its enclosure and crypt-like qualities. Thus "this" becomes an all-inclusive counter-trope which recognizes, a priori, its futile mission to represent all absence. And like the bodiless serpent which flashes without a skin or the shoe of glass that fits but is never seen, the "this" is first the intimation that the *Auroras* will celebrate absence, formlessness, and the memories of presences that never were.

Stevens' serpent, or the auroras poematized, is like the

death-muse and the Cinderella trace: all are the residue of an imagined absence or what the poet had called "the inconceivable idea of the su(o)n." For as summer turns to autumn in the *Collected Poems*, the sun and serpent of *Ideas of Order* also undergo a haunting; what remains of the sun is the shivering residue of its auroras and what remains of the self is the fiction of the serpent which becomes the metaphallic bridge between this world and that ghostlier one. That ghostlier world is cast as the "end of the cave" where consummation is death and death, consummation. The compression in these passages is Stevens at his most intense. Cave and grave, muse and mother, poet and son, text and crypt, all converge at the opening of the *Auroras* so that the poet may bid them farewell: that is to finally recognize them as fictions that never were. This is his poison; that even a death trope is a fiction of the ultimate which repeats the fixations of the origins of birth and life. There are actually three serpents imposed on the opening of the poem: the flecked animal moving in the grass of childhood, "the master of the maze" which triumphs over the repetitive "forms and images of life," and finally the aurora serpent whose life is absence, another "bodiless' for "the body's slough." All three, at the end of the passage, remain intertwined and connected in an endless chain signifying the poet's quest for a presence and a poetry that will never suffice.

The serpent chain of the first canto tends to encircle the entire meditation on the auroras for as Stevens writes in the concluding stanza, the poem is a "turn back to where we began;" to turn back to where we began is to trope on the fictions of origins, the fortunate fall, the mother's face, the father sitting in space. In Cantos II, III, and IV, the three serpents in this fictive 'chain of being' unfold into the ghostly absences that were the imagination (II), and muse (III) and father-principle or the poet dreamer who says "no to no and yes to yes." These were the ideas that ordered the poet's memory, and now, as he bids them "farewell," the illusion of order is dissolved, these centers do not hold, and the only "idea" which is left to exist is memory's turning in absence.

Stevens had written in an earlier lyric on "The American Sublime," that the vision of the sublime is one of blinking and blankness, of "the empty spirit in vacant space."[10] Canto II repeats the vision of that questor after the sublime and his gaze into the abyss:

> Farewell to an idea . . . A cabin stands,
> Deserted, on a beach. It is white,
> and by custom or according to
>
> An ancestral theme or as a consequence
> Of an infinite course. The flowers against the wall
> Are white, a little dried, a kind of mark
>
> Reminding, trying to remind, of a white
> That was different, something else, last year
> Or before, not the white of an aging afternoon,
>
> Whether fresher or duller, whether of winter cloud
> Or of winter sky, from horizon to horizon.
> The wind is blowing the sand across the floor.
>
> Here, being visible is being white
> Is being of the solid of white, the accomplishment
> Of an extremist in an exercise . . .
>
> The season changes. A cold wind chills the beach.
> The long lines grow longer, emptier,
> A darkness gathers though it does not fall
>
> And the whiteness grows less vivid on the wall.
> The man who is walking turns blankly on the sand.
> He observes how the north is always enlarging the
> change,
>
> With its frigid brilliances, its red-blue sweeps
> and gusts of great enkindlings, its polar green
> The color ice and fire and solitude. (*CP*, 412–13).

In the three cantos which follow on the serpentine

chain, there is a sense of letting go or release from the ideas of presence that have dominated the poems from the beginning. As he turns from the serpent of childhood to the seascape with its deserted cabin, Stevens takes up what I will call the "white mythology" of the American sublime, or the centrality of the vision that links the fiction of the sublime moment with the visible absence of color: white. The most obvious percursor to this topos of whiteness is Melville who identifies the white whale with the thought of annihilation not only of nature but of the "self." In his reading of the whiteness of Melville's whale, John Irwin suggests that it is the indefiniteness of this noncolor and its ability to represent the "truth" about the external world (that it is an abyss), which haunts the sublime questor in the American landscape.[11]

> With the loss of belief in an external absolute, the self expands to fill the void, but at the moment when the self becomes the absolute, at the moment when it sees that everything is a projection of itself, then the self realizes it has become nothing, that it is indistinguishable, "a colorless all-color." Hawthorne speaks of that "disordered mental state," . . . when a man, rendered morbidly self contemplative extends "his egotism over the whole expanse of nature."[12]

Stevens' turning to the white cabin with its decorations of white flowers and its backdrop of winter white clouds moves Irwin's text of the American egotistical sublime one step beyond. For the sublime questor in Stevens knows that the self's gesture to expand its egotism over "the expanse of nature" is a fable of freedom based on the predication of an absent self. Instead of focusing on the fictional dialectic between internal and external absolutes or even the artifice of annihilation which appalls his poetic precursors, Stevens invents a twentieth century version of the American sublime that posits the fiction of the family romance as the indefinite and infinite whiteness that haunts the vestiges of our memories.

Stevens' cabin, or the idea of a cabin, is a trope for the illusion of the scene or origin that has already been emptied (deserted) and effaced by the contamination of memory. Memory's retracing toward such a scene is always whitewashed, not only by the passage of time and, as the poet writes, by the infinite course of the life, but also by the impossibility of entry into a place or time that only exists as an invisible (white) idea.

What does remain is the trace of that forbidden sexuality that adds prescience to our dreams; and that trace is figured here not by the white flower invisible against the whiteness of the cabin but by its withered edges that are the vestiges of the abandoned Eden. The edges of the flowers against the wall are, as Stevens writes, a "kind of mark" or hieroglyph, which, like the scribblings on the hulk of the white whale, are the markings which signify the impossible access to the primal union between self and other, inside/outside (nature) or whales and humans. And yet, those withered edges that mark these disjunctions displace the primal whiteness to become a postlapsarian scene from which stranger fictions are made. Those fictions, which become in the *Auroras of Autumn* the fictions of absence, begin with the poet's entry into the forbidden primal chamber where tropes of nature as external absolute have taken over the snowy cabin. As the wind blows the sand across the floor in a repossession of the human house, the sublime questor envisions himself as invisible, as part of nature and not part of himself; but that very nature which excludes him tends to mark him and make him more visible than before. This extremist in the sublime exercise discovers that the fictions of absence are identical with the fictions of presence, both the constructs of a rhetoric that accomplishes nothing but a silencing.

And so, as he moves away from the blank whiteness encountered in the erasure of the scene of origin, the season changes, the beach is now emptier than before and the blinding whiteness is neutralized by "the red-blue sweeps" of the actual auroras. Perhaps the most dominant image of presence for Stevens had always been "the mother's face," not, as Harold Bloom erroneously suggests, Stevens' actual mother, but the mother's face as figure for the origin of primal vision where poetry begins.[13] Canto III is another saying of farewell that begins as a reenactment of a spectacle of memory that tries to represent the preconscious, visual, and preverbal stage when the mother's face is one's own:

> Farewell to an idea . . . The mother's face,
> The purpose of the poem, fills the room.
> They are together here, and it is warm,
> With none of the prescience of oncoming dreams

In this imaging of his own conception, the poet finds an entrance into origins through the face of the mother or the idea of the mother's face. The dream begins *in utero* where the illusion is created of a womb of art, and the suggestion is made that the purpose of the poem is the disclosure of its own origins. However, as most readers of twentieth-century poetry know, this dream of regression gestures not so much toward the womb as origin but toward that repetitive flight from unpleasure which Freud linked with the death instinct.[14] Thus this passage is informed by the problematic of repression that becomes a forgetting of the mother's face as death mask or ultimate end instead of beginning, and an undoing of the preconscious state as beginning but rather ultimate repose.

The fiction of primal union figured in the first stanza where "They are together and it is warm" begins to dissolve in the following four lines when the poet, now not an infant but the inhabitant of "the house of evening" recognizes that even in his imagining of the parental union something has been consumed and obliterated; disjunction or what the poet refers to as "halfness," or what contemporary theorists name as otherness is ever present even at the moment of imagined sublimity: "the half they can never possess remains." Here the poet refers to an inheritance of absence that is always a subtracted constant in the attempt to find wholeness. For the poet's own troping is a repetition of the parent's troping on an absence that is always the mother's face. The phantom of the mother, as trace, is the endless duplication mirrored in the invention of the interior paramour who never takes her place. However, she too is now dissolved and consumed as "she gives transparence" (transparents). But she has grown old. The necklace is a carving not a kiss. Where once the word "transparence" in Stevens was associated with the illusion of primary essence and disclosure, it can now be linked with the idea of parental connections or tropological crossings that occur between parents and children or poets and paramours. The gift of the mother, then, is not her kiss, but her trace, the necklace, that occasions the possibility of troping and peace of the present moment.

The four stanzas following the dissolution of the mother are a study in metonymic reversal in which the object stands for its function, even though such an inversion does not threaten the rhetorical essence of the trope. The soft hands, the house, and books begin to collapse and return to a place where language lives in an abyss. Nature too is transmuted and appears like something it is not, "when boreal night will look like frost as it approaches them." Trope is nature and nature trope, as the poet bids goodnight to his muse and she falls asleep. The "delicious word" of this death mother is not only goodnight but death, and that final moment is signaled when boreal night shines on the window front of the poet's consciousness and cannot enter his room. Nature itself has become a theatre of trope when all is envisioned as outside and refracted, mirror within mirror; and, when nature takes over completely, "only the windows will be lighted, not the rooms." The effect of this uncanny moment is not mediated by Stevens' vision of the end, for the last word is the wind's that sweeps away the sounds of language and orders the mother's face to its command.

The *Aurora of Autumn*'s three attempts to say goodbye to the fictions of presence are answered by three deconstructions which negate the command of the wind and its "invincible sound." As he turns to the principle of the father, which as Geoffrey Hartman correctly asserts, always arises within the maternal sphere, the poet affirms the masculine principle but with some hint of cancelling as indicated in the words "as one that is strong."[15] Stevens' *Aurora's* father is an Old Testament patriarch whose visage does not have the gentlest aspects of the mother's face and is marked by "the bushes of his eyes." This image that barely emerges out of nature also suggests the burning bush that will not be consumed and perpetuates the notion of the father as the idea of order, morality, and voicing. However, the potency of the father principle is consistently undermined in this canto, because even his power of voicing is an intoning through repetition, the utterances of the mother. The cosmic power that the father once possessed, that "voice in the whirlwind," and the potential that could leap from "heaven to hell in flames" is now reduced to a "green thought in a green shade." He is silenced and has returned to the state of nature waiting to hear the approach of a new company of actors. But the father who would put on the mask of the actor is cautioned to look on his present throne not as the principality of time and space but a spectacle that ultimately is only a theatre of trope. Stevens seems to be saying that man masks himself in the fictions of authority (and also his gods) but his angels' flights are unmasked by the wind itself or the fiction we call the unnameable outside.

The canon's revision of the family romance reaches its peak in the Canto V of the *Auroras* where mother, father, mistresses, and son take up a frenzied masque in which mother plays nature, father is poet, and son announces himself as agonistic ephebe. The function of the mother in this absurd theatre is to nurture and "invite humanity to her house and table." But her consort, the poet, is silenced by the generosity of her gesture, and in his anxiety, sublimates by fetching "tellers of tales" or proliferating fictions that demystify the maternal mystery. He protects his children (poems) by veiling the maternal abyss with fictions or those "negresses who dance among the children." These latest guises of the paramour distract the children, who, through the agency of the benign father, turn away from the void. The object of the masque is to depict the bequest of the father, who, as belated Prospero, perpetuates the Nietzschean lie that truth is falsity and fictions are true. In the last two stanzas, the father is confronted by his agonistic son who would uncover the lie and lift the veil that covers poetry as a theatre of trope. One would expect the reverse; that it would be the father who lifts the veil to disclose the baselessness of his fictions.

> What festival? This loud, disordered mooch?
> These hospitaliers? These brute-like guests?
> These musicians dubbing at a tragedy,
>
> A-dub, a-dub, which is made up of this:
> That there are no lines to speak? There is no play.
> Or the persons act merely by being there.

The ephebe's questioning of the father's festival discloses the son's ability to perceive the muteness behind the effort: poetry "mutes much" in its forgetting that the spectacle is an illusion and "muses much" or tropes on the muteness it unveils. As the canto ends, the theatre (like the cabin in canto II) is emptied out, and, by the end of the next canto, even the theatre of *Notes Towards a Supreme Fiction* dissolves into the image of a cloud. The emptied theatre persists in the *Aurora*'s volume as the poet's metaphor for poverty; but poverty in the later poetry is not the destitution of imaginative desire but rather "the heart's strong core" or knowledge that the abyss is what sustains the poet's abysmal melodies.

The metaphoricity of the theatre and the fictions of the self that it has engendered enter within the crematorium of memory in canto VI. In this most sublime passage of the

Auroras (sublime in the old Longinian sense of the word), the poet presides over the holocaust of his own memory in which all naming, fictive selves and even the imagined primal scene are burned. Before, in canto II, the effacing of the cabin with its flowers as memory-traces, was merely a whitewashing or incomplete erasure of absent fictions. As memory disclosed the terror of its own blankness, its fictive traces reappeared in the formation of visible hieroglyphs of the inside.

Now the fear and trembling experienced by the fiction of the poetic ego in this canto are troped into a return through vanishing corridors and collapsing capitols to a primal moment where all is destroyed by flames. The parental space that so haunted the sublime questor of the first few cantos is in flame: it is a moment of devastation and dispossession in which memory itself is seemingly obliterated and with it the fictions of the parents, the self and its origins.

> . . . He opens the door of his house
> On flames. The scholar of one candle sees
> An artic effulgence flaring on the frame
> Of everything he is. And he feels afraid.

This fiction of the moment of negative subliminity, when Other and poet are so estranged that nature threatens annihilation, is ultimately both the sublime as suicide and as salvation. For the poet is again confronted with the whiteness of the abyss that is both the knowledge of nothingness (inside and out) and the mythology of whiteness that makes possible the figuration of the abyss. With the conflagration of the absent primal scene that has been an unnaming of a nameless thing, the poem moves toward another figurative nexus in which, now purged, the construct of imagination pauses to contemplate its own absence or death. It asks: What is this reflected light that makes possible both the luminosity of the auroral night and the reflections of an absent self in the illusions created by metaphor. The mystery of both uncanny replications is subsumed by the familiar Stevensian notion of the trace or "shivering residue." That trace, the shoe of glass that is visible and invisible or both, is the trope synecdoche or that "part of the world" that may be figured forth in poetry.

Memory returns in canto VII to play with that trace of the nameless that remains, and in this play, the poet returns to the notion of halfness that is always present in the parental embrace. That halfness is apparent too in a language which tries to posit its own absence and fails. For language cannot, in the midst of summer pause to imagine winter, for the naming of summer is already an unmaking in its proleptic disclosure of the absent season winter. In naming, the canto suggests, language unmakes what it tries to name. All, then, is merely a "flippant communication under the moon."

With the poem's exhaustion of the power of language to refer to anything besides itself, cantos VIII through X reaffirm the centrality of language in this poem of the American sublime. Language has the power to move us, even though what it creates are fictions and not essences of presence or "the empty spirit in vacant space." Textuality is like a book at evening beautiful but untrue"; and yet that which the text invents cannot be evaluated within the categories of truth and lying—as it is, it is, untrue.

One is able to be poet if he represses the knowledge of true and false constructs, if he lives with the philosophy of "as if" and substitutes the fiction of the auroras for the auroras themselves. Christian mythology posits that there will be "a time of innocence" when we will lie "in the quiet of sleep" with our messiah; but the bread and wine of this belated poet are his theaters of trope that make possible, even as predicate, a time when innocence will come true. The dymystification of Christianity that occurs in canto VIII opens up the possibility of another false messiah, the troping poet, whose yea-saying makes possible a time of innocence that exists as idea—as it is, it is.

This canto too takes up the reconstruction of a new

primal scene where we are back to another first warmth and the fiction of an "inocent mother" singing in the dark of memory's room. This uncontaminated maternal presence, a virgin Mary, who creates a time and place of innocence, arises from the holocaust of memory in canto VI as the trace of the original primal scene is erased. If the first primal scene posited the "mother's face" as purpose of the poem, this revisionary passage is not only an unnaming of the face as originating synecoche, but a radical reading of the scene itself in which there is no father or union but only the voice of the mother—"half heard." The displacement of the father or Oedipal undoing in the scene of the mother and child is trope which is a forgetting of the dream of sexuality or the repression of the primal abyss.

The memory of an innocent primal scene leads into canto XI and its illusory erasure of guilty dreams.

> We were as Danes in Denmark all day long
> And knew each other well, hale-hearted landsmen,
> For whom the outlandish was another day
> Of the week, queerer than Sunday.

The decentering of the father is perpetuated in these lines where all males are brothers or the fictive siblings of the self. We are reminded too of Hamlet in Denmark who would desexualize his mother and make her immaculate. This vision of the brothers, doublings of the fictive self, fattening themselves on a decorous honeycomb to eventually "lie sticky with sleep" is an uncharacteristically graphic image for Stevens: however the stongest reading of these lines is as an autoerotic phantasy that dramatizes the narcissistic reflections of a text that cannot make connection with the mother's face or voice but only with itself.

The poet's own uneasiness with this little drama of the activity of poetic fate is troped into the familiar topos of the poet and his paramour and their "intensest rendezvous." The fiction of the female is reallowed because ultimately, as the doubled beloved of the poet's self, she offers more possibilities than either hale-hearted landsman or dispossesed father. But the female also brings with her the shadow of death, that "may come tomorrow in the simplest word." By the end of canto IX, we have turned back to where we began, as Freud's "old man yearns in vain for the love of a woman as he had it first from his mother." As the serpent chain begins to conclude its encircling of the meditation on the auroras, the tracings of memory have been consumed. We are reborn to innocence, this poem would like to believe, to that preconscious stage that succeeds and precedes the traces of consciousness.

Wallace Stevens was not content to leave this poem of absence in such a mood of reconstructed bliss: instead, his last stanza makes mockery of those readers (rabbis) who endow language with the possibility of disclosure or who would try to read meaning in nature as external absolute. Those contrivers of the sublime mode, "contriving balance to contrive a whole," are, like Emerson, "a [deluded] happy people in a happy world." "Death's own supremest images" are compounded by a sublime questor thwarted by "the spectre of the spheres" who knows, in advance, the absolute of the dumbfounding abyss. The vision at the conclusion of the poem is not of a spinning Cinderella fulfilling herself under the roof of trope, but of a "hall harridan," Cinderella's stepmother, who whispers the words of the third woman . . . "death, death, death."

Notes

1. All references to Stevens' poems are from Wallace Stevens, *The Collected Poems* (New York: Knopf, 1961), hereafter cited as *CP*. The allusion to the "interior paramour" is in "Final Soliloquy of the Interior Paramour," *CP*, 524.

2. J. Hillis Miller, "Stevens 'Rock' and Criticism as Cure," *Georgia Review* XXX (1976), 5–31.

3. Harold Bloom, *Wallace Stevens: The Poems of Our Climate* (Ithaca: Cornell University Press, 1976), 359.

4. Michael Beehler, "Stevens' Boundaries," *Wallace Stevens Journal VII:¾ (1983), 99.*

5. *Paul Ricoeur, Freud and Philosophy: An Essay on Interpretation* (New Haven: Yale University Press, 1970), 246.

6. Ibid., 247.

7. See "In the Carolinas," *CP*, 4.

8. Ricoeur, 247.

9. Bloom, 253–280. And Joseph Riddel, "Metaphoric Staging: Stevens' Beginning Again of the "End of the Book" in *Wallace Stevens: A Celebration*, edited by Frank Doggett and Robert Buttel (Princeton: Princeton University Press, 1980), 308–339.

10. "American Sublime" *CP*, 130.

11. John Irwin, *American Hieroglyphics* (Baltimore: Johns Hopkins University Press, 1982), 257.

12. Ibid., 258.

13. Bloom, 255.

14. See Sigmund Freud, *Beyond the Pleasure Principle*, translated, edited James Strachey (New York: W. W. Norton Company, 1961).

15. Geoffrey Hartman, *Saving the Text* (Baltimore: Johns Hopkins University Press, 1981), 278.

Chapter 8

In the Twilight of the Gods: Women Poets and The American Sublime

JOANNE FEIT DIEHL

> *Then we,*
> *As we beheld her striding there alone,*
> *knew that there never was a world for her*
> *Except the one she sang and singing, made*
> *--Wallace Stevens*

Emerson, the father of the American sublime, writing in 1844, revels in the possibilities of the power that emanates from new men in a new land, a power that has its source in abandonment to "the nature of things," in an ecstasy of release:

> It is a secret which every intellectual man quickly learns, that beyond the energy of his possessed and conscious intellect he is capable of a new energy (as of an intellect doubled on itself), by abandonment to the nature of things; that beside his privacy of power as an individual man, there is a great public power on which he can draw, by unlocking, at all risks, his human doors, and suffering the ethereal tides to roll and circulate through him; then he is

> caught up into the life of the Universe, his speech is thunder, his thought is law, and his words are universally intelligible as the plants and animals.[2]

Transformed by the universe flowing through him, the new man experiences the apotheosis of the Emersonian sublime—one with the world, he assumes its authority, his speech achieving the clarity of cosmic law. Implicit in this wondrous transformation is Emerson's faith in the self's ability to open doors, experience the flood, and speak with a voice of thunder in language bold as it is clear, a language where sign and signification are one. Yet Emerson's assertion presents difficulties not easily overcome by poets of lesser confidence or by those who lack the support of a tradition, even if it be one Emerson himself would advise the new man to discard. Women poets experience the burden of these difficulties in ways that bar their free access to the sublime, for gender blocks the identifications Emerson so fluently assumes. If the principle of desire governs the subject's reaching for fulfillment in the sublime, then the sublime finds its origins in the realm of eros. Thus, the relation of sexual identity to the quest for the sublime reveals the woman poet's provisional status within the romantic literary tradition.

Translated into psychosexual terms, the tensions of the experiential sublime have recently been most clearly articulated by Bruce Clarke:

> Sublimity is psychologically cognate with the structure of desire and its repression: it is the mark of the momentary intense experience of a discontinuity between desire and the possibility of its fulfillment. Sublimation occurs on either side of this moment: it pertains to the status quo disrupted by the sublime encounter, and consequent upon this disruption works toward the reinstatement of a renewed, although possibly altered, equilibrium. . . . The sublime tends to accentuate disparities, or to create them; it tends to break continuities and open epistemological gaps—it is the creature of duality. . . . Sublimity is general-

> ly the preferred term for great poetry or great experience; it is the attribute of those moments of confrontation, risk, trial, or terror, at which point one's great lessons are learned. Yet efficacy of sublimation will determine our relative ability to convert the experience of sublimity into daily use.[3]

In the play of desire and its repression, in the currents between sublimation and the sublime, Clarke finds the strength of the Wordsworthian imagination, and, I would venture, the tradition of a naturalizing Romanticism. Women poets, however, experience difficulty in achieving access to this sublime because in order to withstand the accentuated disparities, the breaking up of continuities, and the re-creation of an experiential duality, the poet must have faith that he/she retains the capacity to survive such an upheaval intact—either that the self will reassert its power after the tide of spirit has ebbed, or that the external power is experienced as being related to the self, and so possession, in some hidden way, becomes a repossession of uncharted regions of the self.[4] The poet, furthermore, must believe that he can find within not only the restitutive capacity for survival, but the ability to call forth language adequate to the experience he has undergone. As Emerson assures us, the poet thus speaks for all men, although paradoxically, (and such paradoxes lie at the heart of the experiential sublime), the internal power he discovers depends on the energies of the world.

But the woman poet does not, in the nineteenth century, or for that matter in the early twentieth century, perceive herself as speaking for commonal experience, as "representative." Instead, women poets more often perceive themselves as exceptions, as isolates, departing from, rather than building upon a tradition. Thus, when the external power floods into the self, so that the self must momentarily fall away, the subject experiences no assurance either that this influx of power shares her identity or that the sublime encounter, once undergone, will prove emblematic for a whole company of poets, or prove true for womankind s a recognizable emergent tradition. Thus, the woman poet is particularly susceptible to the dangers of a momentary discontinuity such as Clarke describes, for it severs her from the origins as well as the fulfillment of her desire by rendering her passive in literary as well as in biographical terms. The woman poet who possesses an independent, heterodox intellect would be wary of such experience, dreading its power to usurp her energies as she acknowledges the crucial nature of the sublime encounter itself.

In more explicitly Freudian terms, Thomas Weiskel describes the oedipal interactions at the heart of the romantic sublime, an experience that threatens to vanquish the poet as it challenges the autonomous imagination. This sense of threat, Weiskel notes, fades when the poet can recognize the identity between himself and the engulfing other (an identity, I would add, that women poets cannot simply assume).

> The fantasy of injury ends in the simultaneous perception of defeat and the realization that the threat is not, after all, a real one. This makes possible a positive resolution of the anxiety in the delight of the third phase, which is psychologically an identification with the superior power.[5]

This reconciliation won by poets who survive to write of the sublime presents the crux of the difficulty for women. Traditionally, the superior power can be either the image of patriarchal authority whose spirit in Freudian terms would merge with the Father's or, for the poets of a naturalizing romanticism, that spirit could be perceived as feminine, the Mother Nature who weds as she nurtures her son. Indeed, this second pattern, with its carefully modulated violation of the incest taboo; defends against a too literal psychosexual examination of the workings of the romantic sublime. Yet it is just here that women poets encounter their major conflict with the traditional manifestations of the sublime experience, difficulties which threaten to cut them off from the test of sublimity—from achieving the poetry of grandeur and consummation that draws on a power greater than that found in the conscious self alone. If this vision of power describes the conscious imagination's experience of unconscious forces, then the question becomes how women's experience of the unconscious redefines rhetorical forms. But I wish here to stay within the realm of an idealizing poetics, and thus speculate that women poets must redefine their relationship to this Authority as they have had to reimagine their relationships with their poetic precursors. As Weiskel shows us, the workings of poetic influence and the experience of the sublime are intimately related and often merge into a single phenomenon when that external presence finds its authority in an earlier poet.[6]

Consider the possibilities—if authority is associated with the patriarch, then the woman poet cannot so easily experience the identity between self and all-powerful other; instead, his presence may seem so "ravishing" (a term long associated with the workings of the sublime), that she is vanquished. As avatar of the patriarch, his power remains external to hers, for she is not the son who joins that male company of descendental poets known as poetic tradition. If, on the other hand, the woman poet experiences this external power as feminine, as the mother, her "inspiration" does not impart the gift of tradition. Instead, the woman poet develops an alternative line of descent where the maternal image coincides with poetic identity. This matriarchal genealogy—although promising future power—remains largely nascent in the nineteenth century, the power of the poet/mother yet to be freed. Consequently, verbal inspiration may be tentatively identified by the woman poet with maternal/natural forces, an identification that carries with it an aura of the heterodox and hence a quality of subversion, resulting from the disrupted canonical relationship of poet to muse. The male poet resolves his difficulties—the terrifying discontinuity in his selfhood—by aligning himself with the culturally assumed identity of the patriarchal voices of authority, thus at once reclaiming his own superiority without denying his access to the reciprocal relationship between the imagination and the natural world. Not so, the woman poet. Faced with an overdeterminacy born of a relationship where her position as passive, receptive self mirrors her culturally assumed identity, a relationship where the authoritative power *is* the masculine other, she becomes either silenced by the incursions of the sublime or radicalized by the process. But before investigating the relations of women poets to the American sublime, I return to the tradition's origins, to the conditions of the soil that create the spirit of poetry in the wilderness.

II

The imagination whose power initially shapes the tradition of the American sublime is, of course, Emerson's and it is to his conception of the sublime that I return. Critics have rightly emphasized the Orphic power of the Emersonian sublime, its regenerative and liberating aspects. If one views the American sublime from an antithetical vantage point, however, other, more disturbing qualities appear which illuminate the severely exclusionary character of this tradition for women poets, exiled by definition from apprehensions of the native sublime and banished from their traditional social sphere of domesticity. Emerson's sweeping gesture of inclusiveness, his great incursion of power into the Me, incorporates both male and female identities and appropriates the language of the home to describe male consciousness. Emerson's vision of the Poet does more, however, than simply relegate the domestic world to the province of men. Following his Romantic fathers, Emerson claims the domestic sphere for the poet and finds in the ordinary, in household implements and daily physical experience, the groundwork of the sublime.

> I embrace the common, I explore and sit at the feet of the familiar, the low. Give me insight into today, and you may have the antique and future worlds. What would we really know the meaning of? The meal in the firkin; the milk in the pan; the ballad in the street; the news of the boat; the glance of the eye; the form and the gait of the body;—show me the ultimate reason of these matters; show me the sublime presence of the highest spiritual cause lurking as always it does lurk, in these suburbs and extremities of nature[7]

Such an assertion apparently offers both men and women renewed access to the origins of the experiential sublime, divorcing sublimity from the exotic, the terrifying, the strange; and severing its ties from the gothic imagination to which it had historically been so closely allied. This advantageous revision (particularly for women both as victims in the gothic and as dominant presence in the house) becomes starkly modified, however, when Emerson moves from the world of things to a landscape of persons. For here the domestic world of dailiness quickly becomes an enemy of the single soul's quest for the sublime when the knot of family affections threatens to shatter the requisite solitude of the individual, thus upsetting the possibilities of apprehending the Oversoul.

If Emerson laments the ruins of the affective life, he cannot satisfactorily resolve the conflict, and it remains to haunt him through this last years. When they stand in the way of the "great and crescive self," the soul rejects family ties, and turns its attentions eclusively within.[8] "I shun father and mother and wife and brother when my genius calls me."[9] Such whim is not, of course, without its human implications, implications which force a choice between the mediating aspects of personal relationships and the sublime experience of the self's union with the oversoul, unencumbered by any other human presence. Incorporating domesticity within the self as subject, the me further severs the possibility of family ties and the discrete balancings of friendship to attend to the solitary imagination's enterprise. Thus women are doubly excluded from Emerson's poetic program—they are neither required for the domestic sphere (recall *Walden*, Thoreau's project of celibate domesticity), nor are they needed to fulfill the male's desire in the realm of the imagination. As Emerson identifies the poet with Christ, or the resurrection of an ancient bard, his ancestors as well as his origins reassert their patriarchal associations. Although this identification is certainly not new in Emerson, its force renders his poetic vision intensely exclusionary and dominated by male presence.

Even more severely than in British Romanticism, American Romanticism consequently displaces the woman from poetic identity. Marriage between mind and nature no longer serves as the primary model for imaginative celebration; instead, the Wordsworthian epithalamian fades before the acquisitive demands of the Intellect ("marriage [in what is called the spiritual world] is impossible, because of the inequality between every subject and every object").[10] If such a vision leads Emerson to the brink of despair before a universe which contains only "I and the abyss," he can still potentially revive the powers of the single soul. But woman, apparently barred from identification with the poet as the new Christ, removed from the plane of domestic activity appropriated by men, and denied access to the speaking Soul's affective life, finds herself virtually stripped both of her province and her power. When Emerson searches for an analogic language in which to describe the psychic process of poetic activity to delineate the poet's power, he chooses a myth that entwines heterosexual and vegetative modes of reproduction. The engendering muse (product of heterosexual fantasy) no longer signifies the external force that bestows her blessing on the aspiring poet. Instead, Emerson picks, for his analog, the agaric (the mushroom) which does, of course, shed its seeds but requires no feminine body in which to nurture growth. As Thoreau supplants heterosexual activity with the workings of metamorphosis as a way to abrogate the feminine, so in his use of the fungus metaphor, Emerson bypasses human sexuality as a trope for poetic fertility. Here is Emerson:

> Genius is the activity which repairs the decays of things, whether wholly or partly of a material and finite kind. Nature, through all her kingdoms, insures herself. Nobody cares for planting the poor fungus; so she shakes down from the gills of one agaric countless spores, any one of which, being preserved transmits new billions of spores tomorrow or next day. The new agaric of this hour has a chance which the old one had not. This atom of seed is thrown into a new place, not subject to the accidents which destroyed its parent two rods off. She makes a man; and having brought him to ripe age, she will no longer run the risk of losing this wonder at a blow, but she detaches from him a new self, that the kind may be safe from accidents to which the individual is exposed. So when the soul of the poet has come to ripeness of thought, she detaches and sends away from it its poems or songs,—a fearless, sleepless, deathless progeny, which is not exposed to the accidents of the weary kingdom of time; a fearless, vivacious offspring, clad with wings (such was the virtue of the soul out of which they came) which carry them fast and far, and infix them irrecoverably into the hearts of men[11]

Although the obvious emphasis in Emerson's passage is on the power of the poet's genius to survive the ravages of time, this description of poetic production as a form of natural survival carries within it, like the seeds of the agaric itself, its own sub-text—that of sexual politics—which has signigicant implications for the woman who seeks a place for herself as creator. Although originally the agaric is identified with the feminine principle of nature, sexual identification changes as the seed drops to form new life: "She makes a man." Nature limits her role to a maternal function by paradoxically insuring *asexual* reproduction—she creates the agaric (as male poet) which then goes on to reproduce without the necessity of a female partner. Thus, in the preservation of the initiatory maternal form, Emerson discovers a reassuring means for accommodating the principle of sexuality in a world he determinedly seeks to defeminize; the feminine plays the role of functionary in the latter stages of the agaric's creation, detaching from him a new self. Here, mother nature's active introjection into the agaric's life cycle is to remove and plant again, activities which demand no reciprocal participation on the part of the agaric (this circumstance itself perhaps a cause of male anxiety). In this extended description of poetic immortality, Emerson conjoins the asexual pattern of agaric regeneration and a human, albeit remarkably dephysicalized, myth of procreation. Emerson thus invokes human regeneration as he evades it, keeping before us the image of maternity while developing a paradigm that eschews mature heterosexuality.[12]

Marriage not only fails as a model for poetic propagation but also as a symbol for the mind's relations to other selves. The consequences of such disparity render affective relationships inherently doomed. "All private sympathy is partial. Two human beings are like globes, which can touch only in a point, and whilst they remain in contact all other points of each of the spheres are inert; their turn must also come, and the longer a particular union lasts the more energy of appetancy the parts not in union acquire."[13] So we are drawn away from each other, thrust back on our original confrontation between the Me and the Not Me. When Self communes with the powers outside it, nature alone can be our bride. But even this attenuated marriage metaphor is, throughout Emerson, further qualified, for he distrusts to the point of denying the power of anything beyond the great and crescive self. This tenuous marriage with nature, caged in by doubts and often denied in principle, serves to erase the possibility of any explicitly human mutuality that can survive the incursions of the acquisitive imagination. Instead of denying the process of physical regeneration, Emerson recurrently alters the patterns of relationships so that propagation can occur without recourse to heterosexual activity. So complete is

Emerson's usurpation of sexuality by the intellect that it is easy to overlook its implications for a woman poet as reader of Emerson's text, the reader who finds herself not only excised form his vision of home, family, or sexual intimacy, but severed from the very powers associated with her gender, for "mother" nature is more a benign, elderly godmother than active mate. Sensing the implications of such a dismissal, the woman committed to poetry would struggle to retrieve from the Emersonian conception of the poet fragments applicable to herself.

III

By remaking her world in direct response to Emerson, Dickinson asserts her own poetic authority in the face of the American sublime. In the process of constructing such a poetics, however, Dickinson deepens the potential in Emerson for a competitive relationship between intellect and world. To establish her authority in the face of Emerson's poet, Dickinson creates a conception of poetic authority that re-places her self at the center of a self-made world. Formed as they are by syntactical equivocations and hermetic linguistic strategies, Dickinson's poems shape a response to Emerson's poetics that glows with its own austerity. What marks Dickinson's enabling transformations is her internalization of the conflict between the Emersonian me and the not me. The split self thus seeks, from an internal conflict, to engender a poetics which denies the definitions of commonal discourse as well as the realities of a cultural (and a natural) landscape that would prohibit women from naming their world. Characteristically, Dickinson's poems speak of aftermath or prolepsis, thus winning freedom to define the character of experience. Within the corpus of her poems, the sublime assumes unaccustomed yet hauntingly familiar resemblances, as Dickinson inverts the Emersonian concept of the powerful self's relationship to ecstatic experience. The sublime must incorporate a defense against its own radical discontinuities. And this defense takes the form of responding to the necessity of the influx of external power by denying need, by privileging the process of doing without such a sublime implosion of power, or by making renunciation of that power into a force of equal grandeur—into a counter-sublime. Because the empowering influx of the sublime finds its source in nature or in other human or godlike powers, Dickinson does not differentiate, as had Emerson, between persons and things. All externality represents threat—to be indebted is to be vanquished. Consequently, Dickinson's poems move back and forth, erratically, not symmetrically, from the experience of awe before the world to a rejection of the powers of that world and its inhabitants to affect the self. "Transaction is assisted by no countenance," Dickinson insists, for the imaginative process cannot see its way clear to receive the incursions of external forces of forms.[14] And yet, Dickinson's acknowledgment of the transformative effects of power beyond the self abides:

> I heard, as if I had no Ear
> Until a Vital Word
> Came all the way from Life to me
> And then I knew I heard.
>
> I saw, as if my Eye were on
> Another, till a Thing
> And now I know 'twas Light, because
> It fitted them, came in.
>
> I dwelt, as if Myself were out,
> My Body but within
> Until a Might detected me
> And set my kernel in.
>
> And spirit turned unto the Dust
> 'Old Friend, thou knowest me,'
> And Time went out to tell the News
> And met Eternity (1039).

The transformation that recalls a state of grace, the addition of a new sense, occurs here in the opening stanzas; yet the closing lines refuse to leave this experience free from self-questioning irony. For the Might which looms so large, restoring self to soul, may be related to that other mite, as minute as the kernel it implants. So the spirit communes with the dust, restoring it to life, as time becomes eternity. Coterminus with this bestowal of immortal life is the passage into literal death, the self owing its gratitude to the transformative experience which bestows immortality as it takes away life. This gift is double-edged, demanding a sacrifice that equals mortality itself. The interfusion of a corporeal vocabulary with the concerns of the Soul establishes an aura of physical presence startling in its acuity. Sensation—including the inhalation and exhalation of breath—becomes a mode of discourse through which the poet dramatizes the workings of her imagination. For Dickinson, the "Word made Flesh" (p. 1651) "breathes," taking on the life of the spirit which lives within her. The consequences of this process are most significantly an ellision between bodily processes and intellectual work that perceives the sublime in physical as well as psychological terms. Confrontation with an authoritative natural or intellectual spirit appears in Dickinson's poems as a conflict between a defensive subject and what I have referred to elsewhere as her essential adversary. Her debt (recall "I heard, as if I had no Ear") creates its own defensiveness. In this she shares a perception of the sublime with several other women poets who experience an interfusion of the corporeal with the imaginative realms, women who experience the workings of the sublime as an essential process, but one that carries within it, ironically, the shattering capacity for splitting apart that self. Thus the sublime emerges in Dickinson as a compressed and consolidated mode which does away with discursive narrative, where power, whether from landscape or eternal mind, threatens the poet as it infuses her with its presence (thus underscoring her limitations as it challenges her autonomy).

When, however, the external transformative power is

perceived as feminine, the relationship between Dickinson and the Other momentarily frees itself from the corporeal anxieties that customarily mark such confrontations:

> I think I was enchanted
> When first a sombre Girl—
> I read that Foreign Lady—
> The Dark—felt beautiful—
>
> And whether it was noon at night—
> Or only Heaven—at Noon—
> For very Lunacy of Light
> I had not power to tell
>
> — —
>
> I could not have defined the change—
> Conversion of the Mind
> Like Sanctifying in the Soul—
> Is witnessed—not explained—
>
> 'Twas a Divine Insanity—
> The Danger to be Sane
> Should I again experience—
> 'Tis Antidote to turn—
>
> To Tomes of solid Witchcraft—
> Magicians be asleep—
> But Magic—hath an Element
> Like Deity—to keep—(593).

The disruption of perceived experience, the heightening of perception itself, the conversion of the mind and sanctification of the soul, even the "Divine Insanity," echo traditional descriptions of the sublime. Yet, here (unusual for Dickinson) the experiential sublime transpires without the burden of indebtedness, the necessity for physical defensiveness, or the chill of competition. Instead, as the closing lines of the poem suggest, changes wrought can be permanent and should the "I" slip back into conventional sanity, the love found in "Tomes of Witchcraft"—the convert mysteries of powerful female magic—will keep her from losing her newly acquired powers. In Dickinson's fusion of bodily sensation and the workings of the mind, her ellision of poetic influence with the process of the experiential sublime, and her re-shaping of the transformative experience through the redemptive possibilities of a woman-to-woman encounter, we discover the seeds of a tradition that will be elaborated by future American women poets who in various ways attempt to apprehend the American sublime.

IV

Among the women poets whose work gestures toward an alternative tradition of the American sublime, I focus here on Adrienne Rich and Elizabeth Bishop and recall their predecessors, H. D. and Marianne Moore, who in divergent ways manifest possibilities for the development of a counter-sublime. Moore's emphasis on the power of sight that controls her work—the recurrent separation of self from subject—points toward a deeper separation between her identity as woman and her poetic voice, a repression which may have been essential for her to continue to write. Wit operates to discipline passion in ways that render her poems radically distanced. Energies of sublimation have so taken over as descriptions replace plot, animals persons, and verbal effects the illusion of spontaneous feeling, that the sublime can only be approached in its most attenuated form. H. D., in her alternative pursuit of the sublime, draws on esoteric tradition, on a vision of the mythological past, that would bestow on the poet originating powers of divinity denied her by a more immediate literary tradition. Antithetical in their approaches, Moore and H. D. both respond to their status as outsiders by internalizing their sense of poetic estrangement; consequently, their rhetorical strategies, divergent as they are, attempt to conceal as much as they seek to disclose. The esoteric, lost and obscure fact, comes to these poets' defense as a way to continue to write in a language they perceive as not wholly their own. Thus, Moore and H. D. devise a poetics of encoded meanings to reclaim figuration for themselves—Moore, by creating a defensive language that bristles with an obscurity as sharp as her abrasive animals, and H. D. by allying herself with Kabbalistic and occult traditions which seek to rediscover the powers of the lost Great Mother. Both poets maneuver their way toward a poetry that can win access to the powers bestowed by the liberated imagination open to the experiential sulime.

The relationship between Moore and her menagerie clarifies the workings of her poetic imagination and tells us something about her esthetic values as well. Moore herself invites the equation of zoological and literary forms. Consider a short poem, "To A Snail":

> If 'compression is the first grace of style,'
> you have it. Contractility is a virtue
> as modesty is a virtue.
> It is not the acquisiion of any one thing
> that is able to adorn,
> or the incidental quality that occurs
> as a concomitant of something well said,
> that we value in style,
> but the principle that is hid:
> in the absence of feet, 'a method of conclusions';
> 'a knowledge of principles,'
> in the curious phenomenon of your occipital horn.[15]

In her recent book on Moore, Bonnie Costello traces the sources of this poem's quotations and allusions (*Demetrius on Style*, "Duns Scotus," William Cowper's "A Snail") and demonstrates Moore's free use of her sources; but the poem is most characteristically Moore's composition in its devotion to what is hidden, the absence which makes the poem distinctive, and the lacunae in meaning which render Moore's poems so often puzzles in hermetic forms.[16] And yet these poems shed their meanings in the guarded wit of language, a language whose function resembles that of the joke which, according to Freud, "*evade[s] restrictions and open[s] sources of pleasure that have become inaccessible.*"[17] Just as Freud relates the workings of the joke to its ability "to evade an external obstacle," so Moore's language functions as if to create through its own tortuous play, a meaning exempt from the claims of conventional interpretation. Toward the end of "His Shield," Moore asserts: "the power of relinquishing/what one would keep; that is freedom." The tension between playful disruption of syntax and associational composition Moore advocates depends on relinquishment, the giving up that bestows freedom. And similarly, when applied to her style, such relinquishment of commonal meaning, replaced as it is by a wit as defensive as its subject, creates a way out, a breaking through boundaries of linguistic convention to reinvent access to original experience. The choice of animal over human as subject, when it occurs as it does so frequently in Moore's poetry, achieves a distancing and provides a necessary disguise through which Moore can articulate her perceptions of self in relation to the world. In this identification with the animal, one discovers unselfconscious sexual identity and a power that evades categories of cultural convention and human stereotypes. Yet the woman inhabits the animal; the unicorn, in the following poem, finds its match in the "lady."

> So wary as to disappear for centuries and reappear,
> yet never to be caught,
> the unicorn has been preserved
> by an unmatched device
> wrought like the work of expert blacksmiths—
> this animal of that one horn
> throwing itself upon which head foremost from a
>   cliff,
> it walks away unharmed;
> . . . .

Thus this strange animal with its miraculous
elusiveness,
has come to be unique,
'impossible to take alive,'
tamed only by a lady inoffensive like itself—
as curiously wild and gentle;[18]
. . . .

The true child of its mother, the unicorn recognizes its family identity, and this identity betrays the qualities Moore would associate with herself. The unicorn, here an object of art, beautifully crafted and rare, is linked to poetry, especially the care Moore takes in its composition. Finally "Sea Unicorns and Land Unicorns" operates as so many of Moore's poems do, obscuring as it describes the physical character of external forms, Costello remarks, "the effect of Moore's poems is always to make her subject (and her poem) unfamiliar, without allowing it to become alien."[19] Such artful evasions, in their ability to overcome suppression and create a language of meaning that breaks conventional modes only intermittently achieves a balance between wit and articulated feeling. Moore's poems do, however, often brilliantly, establish the ground for future poets (such as Elizabeth Bishop) who perform their rhetorical evasions with greater ease so as to address more directly and to greet with fewer quills the powers tha lurk within themselves.

Although employing different poetic means, H. D. similarly points the way toward the development of an eccentric kind of discourse in which the mask functions once again to dis/close identity. I here briefly consider H. D.'s late work, *Trilogy*, which may be taken as indicative of the directions of her poetic project. "The Walls Do Not Fall," the first section of *Trilogy*, couples the priestly functions of the poet (an Emersonian conception) with the necessity for concealment, an act of evasion. Responding to "someone . . . from USA" who wrote H. D., calling a poet's "troubling to try to express world-issues now, . . . 'pathetic,' " she writes: "but if you do not even understand what words say,/how can you expect to pass judgement/on what words conceal?" Threatened by the condescension of ignorance, the poet replies by seeking protection in the use of codes to disguise her meaning, rendering her language as mysterious as that of ancient priestly rituals. "enigmas, rubrics promise as before/protection for the scribe;/he takes precedence of the priest/stands second only to the Pharaoh."[20] To decipher the code, one must be an initiate; the sacred guards its walls from the incursions of modern profanity. Although pursuit of the hieroglyph may cause the poet to lose her way among the potential chaos of the esoteric, the quest is nevertheless worth the risk: "the elixir of life, the philosopher's stone/is yours if you surrender/sterile logic, trivial reason."[21] This pursuit's dark side is the danger of madness, the sacrifice of upturning layers of tradition which have formed an identifiable interpretation of western ontology. The threat of madness Dickinson confronts experiencing a divided self haunts H. D. in her equally subversive poetic encounters. When "depth of the subconscious spews forth/too many incongruent monsters," she must work out of this negation to reaffirm that "even the erratic burnt-out comet/has its peculiar orbit."[22] Thus form exists, pattern appears, in the apparently most disordered movement. Confidence for such an extreme poetic project, the construction of cryptic forms that depend on the reader's willingness to decipher a hermetic language, rests on H. D.'s belief that words conceal meaning:

> they are anagrams, cryotograms,
> little boxes, conditioned
>
> to hatch butterflies.[23]

Against the background of the World War II bombings of London, H.D. sees herself through her poetic revisionism tenuously reconstructing the world. The journey is treacherous, "mined with risks," to echo Adrienne Rich:

we are voyagers, discoverers
of the not-known,

the unrecorded;
we have no map;

possibly we will reach haven,
heaven.[24]

In *Trilogy*, H. D. envisions the virgin mother Mary as enacting this quest. The role of woman as mother, lover, and subversive power who cannot be accommodated into society is deidealized in the poem's closing movements in which H.D. traces her story against the background of the birth of Christ. This woman carries the unwritten book for the future: "the pages, I imagine, are the blank pages/of the unwritten volume of the new."[25] Refusing to be imprisoned in past myths, "she is Psyche, the butterly,/out of the cocoon."[26] Thus, H. D. establishes the foundations for her poetics in the image of the mythic feminine which she identifies with unconscious forces and the power of language. Such a possibility of identification with the powers of the feminine is "No poetic fantasy/but a biological reality," that marks a new beginning.[27] So, it is the woman herself in "The Flowering of the Rod" who in praising the beautiful fragrance rising from the jar the magus has brought to the Christ child does not realize that the fragrance emanates from the life holds: the jar sealed, "the fragrance came from the bundle of myrrh/she held in her arms."[28]

There is in H. D.'s use of myth not only a tendency toward the obscure but a peculiarly luminous quality as well, a kind of leveling effect which places the dailiness of ritual existence above notions of grandeur. This leveling converts myth into a discourse of homeliness, characterized by the minute detail, the physical gesture, the limitations of a single consciousness moving through history. In the midst of a vision, there may occur a moment of forgetfulness when the speaker awakens from the dream that is the poem's progress:

I do not know what I said
or if I said anything,

for before I had time to speak,
I realized I had been dreaming,

that I lay awake now on my bed,
 that the luminous light

was the phosphorescent face
of my little clock

and the faint knocking
was the clock ticking.[29]

We are never very far from this nightstand clock—with its continued demarcation of the ongoing life of the dreamer in H.D.'s evocation of a mythical past made to serve her inner vision. H. D.'s impetus for re-envisioning human history so as to assert the power of the feminine is grounded, as I have been suggesting, in her perception of a world on the brink of apocalyptic destruction because it has ignored the restitutive force of women.[30] The hope for poetry becomes the remaining hope for civilization—a project in the spirit, if radically divergent from, the Emersonian sublime.

Domesticity again becomes the province of women endowed with the mythic stength to make the homely symbolic of the Divine. H. D.'s search for a language that would both purify itself of the accretions of civilization and establish its own encoded meanings is the double project that distinguishes women poets in their search for a counter-sublime. The desire for a purification of language, moreover, links women poets to their male contemporaries in distinguishing a particularly American yearning. In his recent "Purification and Danger I: American Poetry," Geoffrey Hartman describes the telling repercussions of this attempt to rid language of its poetic associations:

> Poets having expelled the old gods, their images, their phraseology—in short, poetic diction—and, having in-

> stituted a more natural diction, the process of purification continues, not so happily, and the purified language proves to be as contaminated as ever. We see that the poetic diction once rejected had extraordinary virtues, including its nonnatural character, its lucid artifice, the "mirror-of-steel uninsistence" (Marianne Moore) by which it made us notice smallest things and ciphered greatest things, and gathered into a few terms, magical, memorable, barely meaningful, the powers of language.[31]

and yet such a quest for purification is not without its compensatory values, creating poems that do not deny but rather seek to reawaken the ear to the modulations of language. There is a distinction, however, between the motives of the dominant tradition's quest for purity and that of women poets who seek a language that will enable them to reestablish their priority over experience. While the tradition of writing poetry in America becomes increasingly one of lamentation, an elegiac voice longing for the once articulate sublime, the woman poet would offer us the possibility for a renewal grounded in her restitutive capacity—the assertion that women writing redress the balance between self and world, their claim a way of overcoming their belatedness in relationship to the established tradition.

Acknowledging H. D.'s importance for her own work, Adrienne Rich chooses a passage from "The Flowering of the Rod" as the epigraph for *The Dream of a Common Language:*

> I go where I love and where I am loved,
> into the snow;
>
> I go to the things I love
> with no thought of duty or pity

Rich's choice of H. D.'s lines is instructive, for in Rich's own work the pull of eros becomes synonymous with the exploration of an alternative poetics. Confronting the problem of how to write poems that will redefine the character of male-dominated figuration, Rich strives to create a poetry governed by the desire of woman for woman that takes as its premise not the "performative" rhetoric espoused by the male poetic tradition, but a language bordering on silence that achieves its impact in the whisper, the power of an almost silent speech. Although their politics differs, Rich's conception of a new language more closely resembles the dominant American move toward a purified poetics than she might care to admit. If silence becomes the goal toward which poetry strives, then figuration itself becomes a burden; fundamental energies that keep poetry alive, as Hartman notes, are in danger of dying out. Yet the companion impulse in Rich's recent work subordinates this desire for silence, as the poet realizes the extent of her revisionary impulse, the need to sift through the hidden stories of women to find relics of meaning. This reassertion of an alternative tradition grounded in the association of woman to woman, both contemporary and historical, is the impetus for poetry to take up its work once again. In her exclusionary feminist poetics, Rich recovers a saving illusion of need, a world where she can originate speech because none has hitherto adequately conveyed the authoritative experience of woman in the world. Like her predecessor, H. D., Rich searches for her authority in exclusively female experience, in an alternative gesture away from the father-son drama of poetic influence to the mother-daughter relationship. As I have argued extensively elsewhere, Rich's project turns against itself when advocating a discourse bordering on silence, for she assumes in many of these same poems a fiercely rhetorical stance which draws on the very tradition she would eschew.[32] Whitman is as much Rich's predecessor as he is the voice inherently performative and imagistic from which she would free herself, but this must always be the plangent irony of poetic indebtedness. As Rich herself acknowledges, her gift for the very image making she is tempted to cast aside, remains her major strength. And this compensatory impulse toward poetic figuration may offer more promise both for her own career and for the future history of women poets than the silence she admires:

> If from time to time I envy
> the pure annunciations of the eye
> . . . .
> what in fact I keep choosing
> are these words, these whispers, conversations
> from which time after time the truth breaks moist
>   and green.[33]

Rich characterizes the transforming experience that restores words to women by describing a process of relinquishment. This cutting off from the groundtone of tradition issues in a transcndence that would require the purification of death. "Power," "Phantasia For Elvira Shatayev," "To A Women Dead In Her Forties," "Paula Becker to Clara Westhoff,"—in these poems, women speak to or from death, loss providing the freedom for renewed possibilities. And yet Rich's poems keep insisting on life, the will to survive. Against this background of loss, Rich imagines a discontinuous transcendence based on the love of woman for woman and her return to maternal origins, the first intimacy any woman knows:

>   two women, eye to eye
> measuring each other's spirit, each other's
> limitless desire,
>   a whole new poetry beginning here.[34]

"Vision" begins for Rich in a reality that recalls Emerson's domestic landscape. Turning from "jargon in a room" to the minute facts of her home ("bits of yarn, calico, and velvet scraps")—materials salvaged for a new quilt—the woman rediscovers the home Emerson had appropriated for himself. This innately conserving and conservative experience re-places woman in the center of the domestic life from which Emerson had figuratively and for the purposes of poetic figuration banished her. "Care," "conservance," attention to the forms of art, the attributes of the quilt-maker, are those of the woman poet who confronts Rich's version of the American sublime.

Woman's "will to mastery," the aspirations of her ego, must face before the artist's absorption into the forms of her art. As Dickinson asserts a poetics that would replace word with world by dissolving the dichotomy essential for image making, so Rich continues to seek a transcendent form that will re-vise the troubling ground of a sublime poetics based on a discourse she perceives as alien both to her ambition and to her experience as woman. Thus, for Rich, purification of language depends on a uni-sexual cathexis that denies men a place in her world. From this initial premise, she adumbrates a poetry that depends on recovery of her origins as woman as she articulates a sublime that reiterates the power of risk in the guise of duty.

V

If poetry itself is bordering on the limits of expressive form, there are, nonetheless, contemporary poets who are masters of these limits, who, in creating the poems of our climate, return us to ourselves. Elizabeth Bishop is such a poet. Although she would have resisted being classified with "women poets" and would undoubtedly have cast a skeptical eye on the sublime, I choose to close my discussion with a comment on her work in relation both to the alternative tradition of women poets and to the American sublime itself. I persevere against such apparent counter-indications, because despite her reticence, Bishop's poems of passionate reserve fuse a capacity for wonder with a clarity of description which make the sublime once again, however tentatively, possible. A description of the methods

Bishop employs to achieve the effects in her poems becomes itself a summary of those strategies devised by her predecessors—women poets who, like Bishop, felt the need to conceal as much as they disclosed. Like Dickinson, Bishop provides her perception, her vision alone in a world that awaits her meaning yet remains resistant to it. If "Brazil," for Dickinson, is the forbidden exotic, it becomes for Bishop her literal, alternative home. The impetus of the exile which paradoxically turned Dickinson into a recluse (her only form of travel), Bishop converts into the vocation of the almost perpetual traveler, whose powers of observation record her telling observations of a world in which she is acutely aware of her surroundings because she is estranged from them. Her poems maintain a distance, insist on keeping people away by the brilliance of their natural images that enact a thematics of loss.[35]

A late poem, "One Art" (whose title conveys the implicit suggestion that the mastery sought over loss in love is intimately related to the control she maintains in her poetry itself) articulates the tension between discipline in life and the force of circumstance.[36] The poem speaks in the tones of the survivor:

> the art of losing isn't hard to master;
> so many things seem filled with the intent
> to be lost that their loss is no disaster.

The poem's opening line with its echo of a folk prescription such as "An apple a day" leads into the specifics of daily loss—of keys, of time—the syntactic parallelism suggesting an evaluative equation of what we immediately recognize as hardly equal realities. Such parallelism, by providing a temporary distraction that draws the reader away from the cumulative force building in the poem functions as a disarming form of humor that undercuts the self-pity otherwise latent in the poem's subject.

> Lose something every day. Accept the fluster

of lost keys, the hour badly spent.
The art of losing isn't hard to master.

The poem presents a series of losses as if to reassure both its author and its reader that control is possible—an ironic gesture that forces on us the tallying of experience cast in the guise of reassurance. By embracing loss, as Emerson had that beautiful necessity, Fate, Bishop casts the illusion of authority over the inexorable series of losses which she must master.

Then practice losing farther, losing faster:
places, and names, and where it was you meant
to travel. None of these will bring disaster.

The race continues between "disaster" and "master" as the losses encompass her mother's watch, houses, cities, two rivers, a continent, and, perhaps, in the future, an intimate friend whom, breaking out of the pattern of inanimate objects, the poem directly addresses:

—Even losing you (the joking voice, a gesture
I love) I shan't have lied. It's evident
the art of losing's not too hard to master
though it may look like (*Write* it!) like disaster.

Here conflict explodes as the verbal deviations from previously established word patterns reflect the price of the speaker's remaining true to her initial assertion that the experience of loss can yield to mastery. In this deceptively direct poem, with a directness that comes to predominate in Bishop's late work, she delineates the relationship between the will and the world. Note the split of "a gesture/I love" across two lines; the profession stands by itself as well as turning back to the beloved gesture. Syntax reveals the pain that the poem has been fighting, since its beginnings, to suppress. Determined on a course of truth-telling that will cover all contingencies, the thought of losing "you" triggers an anxiety with which the poem must wrestle in its final lines. This last time, the refrain varies its form by assuming an evidential structure which challenges as it expresses what has hitherto been taken as a fact known from within the poet's consciousness. Coupled with the addition of "It's evident" is the addition of the adverbial "too" ("It's evident/the art of losing's not too hard to master") which increases the growing tension within the desire to repeat her credo while admitting growing doubts about its accuracy. In the end, the pressure to recapitulate the by-now-threatened refrain betrays itself in the sudden interruption of the closing line by an italicized hand that enforces the completion of the "master"/"disaster" couplet that the poem itself has made, through its formal demands, an inevitable resolution: "the art of losing's not too hard to master/though it may look like (*Write* it!) like disaster." The repetition of "like" postpones ever so fleetingly the final word which hurts all the more. "Disaster's" inevitability ironically recalls the fatalism of such childhood rituals as "he loves me; he loves me not"—in which the child's first words, "he loves me," and the number of petals on the flower determine the game's outcome. In its earlier evocation of folk ritual and in its tight rhyme scheme, where prescribed verbal patterns determine the "disaster" with which the poem concludes, "One Art" reveals an ironic playfulness that works in conjunction with high seriousness, a strategy that proliferates in Bishop's poems.

Despite the disclaimer, qualifications, and play that mark Bishop's poems, there is an ominous quality to her restraint more suggestive than confession, a tenuous apprehension of self moving through seascapes at once mysterious and alien. Her clarity is a descriptive clarity more than a human one. In such a world the sublime would be what is even more strange, what speaks to us of experiences that carry us beyond ourselves to that which lies unidentified within.[37] Bishop thus speaks as an alienated or exiled sensibility. As outsider, she must observe with all her powers so that she can piece together a map, discern a geography. The map she draws chooses to separate self from phenomena (including other persons), although increasingly in the later poems of *Geography III*, and the poems as yet uncollected which she wrote in her last few years, the move is toward the intimate. Indeed, throughout *Geography III*, Bishop moves closer to the intimate than she had in her earlier poems. I wish to conclude my consideration of Bishop and the sublime and bring this essay to a close by citing three poems from her final book, two companion poems which approach the sublime by means of apparently contrasting yet structurally similar experiences, and the third which defines more clearly than any of her other poems, Bishop's relationship to Emerson and his heirs, Whitman and Stevens—the dominant tradition of the American sublime. The antithetical companion poems are "In the Waiting Room" and "The Moose." While not discounting the surface differences of these poems' narratives, nor their very different tenor, I note similarities between these texts which may help us clarify Bishop's apprehension of the sublime and the form in which she articulates her experience.

Both "In the Waiting Room" and "The Moose" center on the self's relation to others, on an interruption in the continuous act of a sublimation which allows us to perserve an ongoing identity. In each instance gestures of unity with what lies outside the self allow identity to reconstitute itself into its accustomed form. The poems delineate this process—a version of the experiential sublime—by related narrative characteristics. "In the Waiting Room," strangers come together, each awaiting his appointment with the dentist. They share the moments (or hours) of anxiety before their turn arrives, yet remain, in their silent apprehension, isolated. Their status as patients is provisional; they are outside waiting to go in. This provisional relationship exists as well between the people on the bus in "The Moose," where travelers share a journey, yet await their arrival at their individual destinations. Over against these provisional interiors, Bishop establishes images of family. The passengers catch glimpses of a woman shaking "a tablecloth/out after supper." Anonymous voices softly floating from the back of the bus (the back of the mind) create a comforting lullaby of conversation that re-tells the history of people's lives. "In the Waiting Room," familial forms assume, as befits the disturbing character of the poem, a more terrifying if displaced guise. While waiting for her aunt to emerge from the dentist's office, Elizabeth reads the *National Geographic* where images of man, woman, and child assume macabre, distorted forms:

> A dead man slung on a pole
> —'Long Pig,' the caption said.
> Babies with pointed heads
> wound round and round with string;
> black, naked women with necks
> wound round and round with wire
> like the necks of light bulbs.
> Their breasts were horrifying.

What is meant to pass the time becomes a rite of passage as the child is led into an abyss of the self she had not recognized as her own:

> Suddenly, from inside,
> came an *oh*! of pain
> —Aunt Consuelo's voice—
> not very loud or long.
> . . . .
> What took me
> completely by surprise
> was that it was *me*:
> my voice, in my mouth.
> Without thinking at all
> I was my foolish aunt,
> I—we—were falling, falling,
> our eyes glued to the cover
> of the *National Geographic*,
> February, 1918.

The child counters the vertigo that accompanies her sense of a faltering selfhood with facts, information about the external world of the present. What has threatened this identity finds at least its proximate cause in the pictorial representation of man, women, and child rendered grotesque. For consolation Elizabeth turns away, away, we surmise, from the memories of her father's death, her mother's madness—a desolation that could, perhaps, remain controlled only if bound (like the babies' heads by the string) in silence. Facts, though harsh, offer comfort in their very externality:

> I said to myself: three days
> and you'll be seven years old.
> I was saying it to stop
> the sensation of falling off
> the round, turning world
> into cold, blue-black space.
> But I felt: you are an I,
> you are an *Elizabeth*
> you are one of *them.*

Afraid of being "one of them," terrified by the connections that link her to others and the identity that makes her herself, she asks:

> What similarities—
> boots, hands, the family voice
> I felt in my throat, or even
> the *National Geographic*
> and those awful hanging breasts—
> held us all together
> or made us all just one?

The child's reserves of language fail to name the character of her sense of bewildering dislocation:

> How—I didn't know any
> word for it—how 'unlikely.'

Nor does the mature poet provide a word adequate to the uncanny sensation, but instead turns outward as the room reflects the child's terror:

> The waiting room was bright
> and too hot. It was sliding
> beneath a big black wave,
> another, and another.

Without explanation the fissure closes: "Then I was back in it."

> . . . .
> The War was on. Outside,
> in Worcester, Massachusetts,
> were night, and slush and cold,
> and it was still the fifth
> of February, 1918.

If there is no resolution to the child's crisis, merely a slipping back into the everyday world, the poem nonetheless reconstitutes that lost selfhood and then re-places it in the world of facts. Indeed, I would suggest that the close of "In the Waiting Room," with its attenuated self and its spare facticity, characterizes Bishop's poems more generally as the turn toward the external which marks the resolution of the child's crisis may reflect Bishop's more universal strategy of employing descriptions of places, surfaces, and discontinuous visual perceptions to protect a self threatened by internal powers she would prefer to keep silent, sublimated in the waiting room.

"The Moose," on the other hand, employs a similar structuring of experience and a disruption of the self but to very different ends: toward a recapturing of the sublime through a wonder born of the strange. Separateness and fusion, the underlying terms of Elizabeth's crisis in the earlier poem, are the issues here as well; only this time the sudden appearance of the animal—unknown, mysterious—affirms in the passengers' response, the combining power of joy, the possibilities for re-union provoked by awe. Not sure whether one travels with a child or with the recollection of childhood imagination, the reader is carried through a night journey away from home, a journey which is "suddenly" interrupted (the word which signalled the estranging dislocation "In the Waiting Room") by the looming moose. Although the moose's appearance interrupts talk "in the old featherbed," with its evocation of childhood security, the animal offers the sanctity of an alternative home:

> Towering, antlerless,
> high as a church,
> homely as a house
> (or, safe as houses).
> A man's voice assures us
> 'Perfectly harmless . . .'
>
> Some of the passengers
> exclaim in whispers,
> childishly, softly,
> 'Sure are big creatures.'
> 'it's awful plain.'
> 'Look! It's a she!'

As awe reawakens their childhood, the passengers note the sex and appearance of the animal who, apparently in no hurry herself, returns their gaze:

> Taking her time,
> she looks the bus over,
> grand, otherworldly,
> Why, why do we feel
> (we all feel) this sweet
> sensation of joy?

Although the question (with its emphasis on unanimity of feeling) goes unanswered, the joy remains a fact. Majestic presence from another world (moose as feminine muse?) fills the passengers with a "sweet sensation"; the animal, female, emerging from darkness, offers a communal, sacred happiness. Yet despite the communal joy, "The Moose" relinquishes the moment as quickly as "In the Waiting Room." Despite the twisting passengers' heads, the animal disappears, its scent replaced by "an acrid/smell of gasoline." The poem's closing lines wipe out the possibility of carrying this moment of joy into the future:

> by craning backward,
> the moose can be seen
> on the moonlit macadam;
> then there's a dim
> smell of moose, an acrid
> smell of gasoline.

Reality imposes itself on us once again as external fact displaces the momentary sublime. Such a relinquishment of the sublime moment, the fading of experience before ongoing reality, characterizes Bishop's other poems as well. Incursions of power into the Me do not enable Bishop either to project herself back onto the world as Emerson would have us do or, in an equally audacious gesture, depend on the self to become her world—Dickinson's antithetical Emersonianism. Instead, loss (the apprehension of the tenuous character of reality and the instability of the Self) distinguishes Bishop's version of the sublime.

Existing within the liminal space between the domestic and the wild, between land and water, Bishop searches for the redemptive possibilities of home. Another poem in *Geography III*, "The End of March," most fully articulates her understanding of the relatinship between the geography of her imagination and the home ground magisterially domesticated by Emerson, Whitman, and Stevens, progenitors of the American sublime. Here her footsteps follow the tracks of these monumental beachcombers who sought evidences of selfhood on their native shores. The opening of Bishop's poem establishes the inhospitable character of both place and weather—not a good day to take a walk: "It was cold and windy, scarcely the day/to take a walk on that long beach./Everything was withdrawn as far as possible,/indrawn"—offering no welcome and granting no access. As forbidding as the weather seems, this very withdrawal enables the poet to place her imprint on a land unencumbered by approaching waves or the opulence of a brilliantly lit shore. In the face of such austere conditions, drawn on by them, Bishop follows tracks: "dog-prints (so big/they were more like lion-prints)," which lead to "lengths and lengths, endless, of wet white string,/looping up to the tide-line, down to the water,/over and over." This shore "line" lures her to

> a thick white snarl, man-size, awash,
> rising on every wave, a sodden ghost,
> falling back, sodden, giving up the ghost. . . .
> A kite string?—But no kite.

The man who has been there before her has vanished into this snarl; he makes his presence felt through absence, a ghost who has given up the ghost. So haunted by this absence, Bishop continues, aiming for the "crooked box" that would be her "proto-dream-house" where she imagines a bliss of solitude, a place for desultory reading and a "lovely diaphanous blue flame"—"A light to read by—perfect! But—impossible." Having to turn back because "the wind was much too cold/even to get that far,/and of course the house was boarded up," she cannot stay in this place or find her home on this shore. The seascape belongs to the Whitman of "Out of the Cradle," and "As I Ebb'd," the dream of habitation to the Stevens of "The Auroras of Autumn":

> Farewell to an idea . . . A cabin stands,
> Deserted, on a beach. It is white,
> As by a custom or according to

An ancestral theme or as a consequence
Of an infinite course.
. . . .
The season changes. A cold wind chills the beach.
The long lines of it grow longer, emptier,
A darkness gathers though it does not fall

And the whiteness grows less vivid on the wall.
The man who is walking turns blankly on the sand.
He observes how the north is always enlarging the
change,

With its frigid brilliances, its blue-red sweeps
and gusts of great enkindlings, its polar green,
The color of ice and fire and solitude.

The "Farewell to an Idea" of "Auroras" is Bishop's rejection as well. The warmth of domestic possibility she sought in the boarded-up house remains an illusion. Seeking a place where she would live alone, Bishop is barred from entry, prevented from participating in the Stevensian sublime of solitude, illumination, and terror:

. . . He opens the door of his house
On flames. The scholar of one candle sees
An Arctic effulgence flaring on the frame
Of everything he is. And he feels afraid.

Turning back from her journey, going only part way to the house which, of course, is "boarded up," Bishop has seen the sun emerge for "just a minute." Yet the origins of warmth and light have been met by a deepening retraction as the stones "threw out long shadows, individual shadows, then pulled them in again." Bishop here evades Whitman's anxiety of demand:

Dazzling and tremendous, how quick it could kill
me,
If I could not now and always send sunrise out of
me.[38]

She obviates his need to combat the power of the sun through his own linguistic performance by herself noting its fall in the west. Now a ghostly presence, the sun formerly walked along the beach, trailing his kite string:

> —a sun who'd walked the beach the last low tide,
> making those big, majestic paw-prints,
> who perhaps had battered a kite out of the sky to
> play with.

No kite, only the string leads to a ghost and the sun's descent. The poem thus creates an absence that affirms the identities of poetic ghosts by describing an abandoned shore which retains the impress of its former inhabitants. By creating this space, evacuating the shore only to witness its ghosts, Bishop finds her way back to her own origins in the American sublime. The tension between Bishop and Emerson, Whitman, and Stevens—the American sublime—leads her to inscribe her distinct geography on the shore, a geography that disdains the radical solipsism which has hitherto characterized the enterprise of poetry in America. The tentative and the provisional when combined with a language of dazzling specificity and ocular brilliance creates poetry that refuses to take up sides—sustained as it is by the skepticism of an imagination educated by loss yet unwilling, despite temptation, to deny the power of the not me.

What distinguishes Bishop's work from the dominant tradition of the American sublime is a loss equivalent to restitution, the enactment of Bishop's "I" as the eye of the traveler or the child, recapturing an innocence that evades the issues of intimate sexuality or the assertion of gender. One discovers in Bishop's poems a map of language where sexuality gives way to an asexual self, making possible a poetry which frees her from the gender-determined role into which she would be cast as a female descendent of the American sublime. Bishop thus escapes being diminished, exiled, or viewed as apart from the tradition because she subtly evades the distinction in Emerson and his agonistic disciples. The poems' prevailing absence of an overt sexual presence which is felt so strongly in Whitman and Stevens, a dismissal of heterosexuality itself, recalls Rich's so different exclusion of the male as a means to re-establish woman's direct relationship to the world she would make her subject. Although in radically divergent ways, the reticent Bishop and the political Rich both respond to the American tradition's denial of woman as poet by reasserting their poetic authority. Bishop and Rich strive to replace themselves as the center of a poetics which defines a counter-sublime that gestures toward an asexual world (Bishop, through her controlled ironies and effaced selfhood, breaking the confines of a sexually determined tradition to discover an authorizing voice that moves beyond gender).

Women poets in America, as I have been suggesting, face specific, shared difficulties as they strive toward apprehension of the sublime. In a tradition that would grant them at best secondary, provisional status in a cosmos that takes as its primary relationship the masculine me to the not me, the woman poet must find another source of power than that so closely identified by Emerson and Whitman with the Adamic self. If an alternative tradition can be delineated, it begins with Dickinson's antithetical reading of Emerson, her transference of his power into a me that vanquishes all beyond it. The elliptical diction, the at times tortured evasions, the search for hidden gnostic meanings, the surface brilliance that deflects analysis, the highly experimental and difficult cast of poetry by American women reflect their individual sense of alienation and, consequently, their need to employ a language that proves its own defense. Theirs is a poetics that rejects the accreted meanings of tradition to quest after forms that will adequately express the voice of the woman as well as the poet. It is, perhaps, a telling irony that two of our best women poets—Rich and Bishop—should attempt to erase heterosexuality from their work, as if only such a severe gesture would provide access to the linguistic priority each wishes to assert. The Adamic self must give way before an alternative authority: for Rich, the woman as both subject and object of desire; for Bishop, the asexual imagination at work on its own. Though apparently so different in their treatment of eros, these strategies reveal the power that the dominant masculine tradition wields over those who are excluded from it. Exclusion breeds exclusion. In the twilight of the gods, Bishop practices what Dickinson and those who followed her also knew—that renunciation alone might enable the woman poet to rekindle her power and so create in her image the brilliance of an American Counter-Sublime.

Notes

1. Wallace Stevens, "The Idea of Order at Key West," *The Collected Poems of Wallace Stevens* (New York: Alfred A. Knopf, 1968), 129.

2. Ralph Waldo Emerson, "The Poet," *Selections from Ralph Waldo Emerson*, edited by Stephen Whicher (Boston: Houghton Mifflin, 1960), 233.

3. Bruce Clarke, "Sublimation and Sublimity in *Home At Grasmere*," *Studies in Romanticism* 19:3 (Fall 1980).

4. The terms themselves in which the eighteenth-century critic, John Dennis, describes the sublime reveal its erotic associations. Dennis remarks that it

> does not so properly persuade us, as it ravishes and transports us, . . . it gives a noble Vigour to a Discourse, an invincible Force, which commits a pleasing Rape upon the very Soul of the Reader; that whenever it breaks out where it ought to do, like the Artillery of Jove, it thunders, blazes, and strikes at once, and shews all the united Force of a Writer.

The discourse of passion is symptomatic of the context in which the tradition of the sublime develops; the pleasing "rape upon the very Soul of the Reader" is foreshadowed by the experience of the poet who, submitting to a force greater than her/himself, in a condition of transport, experiences the sublime moment. (John Dennis, *Works*, II, "Grounds of Criticism," cited in Samuel H. Monk's *The Sublime: A Study of Critical Theories in VIII-Century England* [Ann Arbor: The Unversity of Michigan Press, 1960]).

5. Thomas Weiskel, *The Romantic Sublime* (Baltimore: The Johns Hopkins University Press, 1976), 93.

6. Ibid., 99.

7. Emerson, "The American Scholar," 78.

8. Emerson, "Experience," 269.

9. Emerson, "Self-Reliance," 150.

10. Emerson, "Experience," 269.

11. Emerson, "The Poet," 231–32.

12. For an analysis of Emerson in relation to gender, see Eri Cheyfitz, *The Trans-Parent: Sexual Politics in the Language of Emerson.* Cheyfitz notes the "Masculine bias of Emerson's work aligned to his vision of power, with the presence of the Mother enacting an ironic function that questions the Father's power." (see Cheyfitz, "Preface," xiv.)

13. Emerson, "Experience," 270.

14. Emily Dickinson, *The Complete Poems of Emily Dickinson*, edited by Thomas H. Johnson (Cambridge, Mass.: Belknap Press of Harvard University Press, 1955), II, 571. All future quotations from Dickinson will be followed by the number of the poem in parentheses within the body of the text.

15. Marianne Moore, "His Shield," *The Complete Poems of Marianne Moore* (New York: Macmillan Co., The Viking Press, 1981), 75.

16. See Bonnie Costello, *Marianne Moore: Imaginary Possessions* (Cambridge, Mass. Harvard University Press, 1981), 52–53.

17. Sigmund Freud, "The Purposes of Jokes," *Jokes and Their Relation to The Unconscious*, translated by James Strachey (New York: W. W. Norton & Co., 1963), 103.

18. Moore, "Sea Unicorns and Land Unicorns," 77.

19. Costello, 26.

20. See H. D., *Trilogy* (New York: New Directions, 1973), "Foreword," vi–vii, "The Walls Do Not Fall," 14–15.

21. Ibid., 40.

22. Ibid., 44–45.

23. Ibid., 53.

24. Ibid., 59.

25. H. D., "Tribute to the Angels," 103.

26. Ibid.

27. H. D., "the Flowering of the Rod," 125.

28. Ibid., 172.

29. H. D., "Tribute," 90.

30. As Susan Gubar has remarked: "Seeking a noncoercive vocabulary, a new language that will consecrate what has been desecrated by her culture, H. D. is propelled by the unsatisfied duality between mother and father to reestablish the primacy to the 'feminine' of what masculine culture has relegated as inessential." (See Susan Gubar, "The Echoing Spell of H. D.'s *Trilogy*," in *Shakespeare's Sisters; Feminist Essays on Women Poets*, edited by Sandra M. Gilbert and Susan Gubar [Bloomington: Indiana University Press, 1979], 209.

31. Geoffrey H. Hartman, "Purification and Danger 1: American Poetry," *Criticism in the Wilderness: The Study of Literature Today* (New Haven: Yale University Press, 1980), 132.

32. See Joanne Feit Diehl, "Cartographies of Silence: Rich's Common Language and the Woman Poet," *Feminist Studies* VI:3 (Fall 1980).

33. Adrienne Rich, "Cartographies of Silence," *The Dream of a Common Language: Poems 1974–1977* (New York: W. W. Norton & Co., 1978), 20. All future Rich poems are from this volume.

34. Rich, "Transcendental Etude," 76.

35. As David Kalstone remarks of *Geography III*: "Her 'questions of travel' modulate now, almost imperceptibly, into questions of memory and loss." (See David Kalstone's chapter on Elizabeth Bishop, "Questions of Memory, Questions of Travel," *Five Temperaments* [New York: Oxford University Press, 1977], 35.)

36. Elizabeth Bishop, "One Art," *Geography III* (New York: Farrar, Straus and Giroux, 1976), 40.

37. Commenting on this relationship between the domestic and strange, Helen Vendler writes: "Elizabeth Bishop's poetry of domestication and domesticity depends, in the last analysis, on her equal apprehension of the reserves of mystery which give, in their own way, a joy more strange than the familiar blessings of the world made human." For an interpretation of Bishop's work based on this premise, see "Elizabeth Bishop: Domestication, Domesticity, and the Otherworldly," *Part of Nature, Part of Us* (Cambridge, Mass.: Harvard University Press, 1980), 97–110.

38. Walt Whitman, "Song of Myself," Section 25.

Index